# *Jot That Down*

# *Jot That Down*

## *Featured Essayists*

Zachary Bartels
Timothy J. Beals
Samuel Carbaugh
Jeff Chapman
Robert G. Evenhouse
Susie Finkbeiner
S.D. Grimm
Tracy Groot
Alison Hodgson
Paul Kent
Kenneth Kraegel
Matthew Landrum
Thomas McClurg
Josh Mosey
Amelia Rhodes
A.L. Rogers
Tom Springer
Ellen Stumbo
John Winkelman

*Edited by A.L. Rogers*

*This volume contains several essays developed by featured contributors. The opinions and advice presented in these essays reflects the professional judgment of the writers. These opinions do not necessarily reflect the position of Caffeinated Press or its editors or directors.*

**JOT THAT DOWN: ENCOURAGING ESSAYS FOR NEW WRITERS**



Published by Caffeinated Press, Inc.
3167 Kalamazoo Ave SE, Suite 203
Grand Rapids MI 49508 USA

www.caffeinated-press.com | +1 888 809 1686 | @CafPress

**Project Team:**
A.L. Rogers, *editor*
Jason E. Gillikin, *book developer*
AmyJo Johnson, *marketing lead*

ISBN-13: 978-1-943548-24-8 (print)
ISBN-13: 978-1-943548-25-5 (EPUB)

Library of Congress Control Number:

First Edition: September 2017 | Second Printing: October 2017

Printed in the United States of America
Initial print run by Color House Graphics, Inc., Grand Rapids, MI
Distributed by Caffeinated Press and by Ingram

# CONTENTS

**PART III: Publishing Your Work**

# INTRODUCTION
## *By A.L. Rogers*

When I started writing I never called myself a writer. I was too embarrassed. I was embarrassed to admit all the things I hadn't done. I'd never had anything published. I hadn't finished a novel or even a short story. I'd never written poetry. (Heck, I didn't even know how to *read* poetry.) I didn't have a blog. I didn't keep a journal. (There was no treasure trove of witticisms and insight tucked in a Moleskine on *my* nightstand.) And I couldn't have told you a thing about Hemingway, or Dickens, or Shakespeare.

I was even embarrassed to admit the few things I *had* written.

When I first started writing I wrote short book reviews for the bookstore where I worked. Other staff members wrote some too. We would print them on a small brochure that looked like it was generated by a Microsoft Word template, not unlike the endless flow of brightly colored fliers and sign-up sheets my elementary schooler brings home in his backpack. The brochure included our reviews along with advertisements and sales information. We stuck them in customers' bags at checkout and called it our "News and Reviews," hoping it would garner the store some extra sales. Did that count as writing? I didn't think so.

Eventually, I met the publisher of a local newspaper that had hardly any distribution and zero budget to pay freelance writers. I asked if I could write album reviews (for free) of new CDs. (Remember those?)

My reviews were only a paragraph or two long. The editor I worked with told me I was "Opinionated. Really opinionated."—but ran them anyway. He was a skinny guy with leathery skin. I met him once, at a Subway that was part of a gas station. Our table was only a few feet from the cash register and shelves of cigarettes. He ate quickly, told me I was opinionated, and said there was no money in writing so I should pursue something else. (The subtext being: or you'll end up like me, holding business lunches at a gas-station Subway.)

Those little reviews certainly didn't count, did they? I wasn't a real writer, was I?

After a while, I started to get brave and told people about my reviews. I even showed some to family and friends. The question I got asked, a question I started to hate, "So, what do you really want to write?"

This one locked me up with dread and embarrassment, too. It certainly wasn't album reviews for Mr. Subway that got me out of bed in the morning. No, I wanted to be a science fiction author. I wanted to write the next *Fahrenheit 451*. And I wanted to write comic books. I dreamed of someday getting to pen a story that would actually find its place in the hallowed canon of Spider-Man or the Flash (my two favorites of the time). But what a joke! Telling people that I wanted to write science fiction and comic books felt like a tremendous cliché, just another nerdy guy who wanted to be like Stan Lee or Ray Bradbury. I imagined them laughing me out of the room.

It took me a few years, and it took the encouragement of a few persistent writer-friends, before I fully adopted the label "writer." Have you ever felt this way? Have you ever thought something like:

*I'm not a writer. All I write is my blog and that doesn't really count.*

*I'm not a writer because all I've ever written are some poems and they're so bad I'll never show them to anyone.*

*I'm not a writer because I haven't published anything.*

*I only write for my friends and family. Just some stories for fun. I'm not a* real *writer.*

Stop it. It doesn't matter.

If you've written, then you're a writer. (Trust me. I had to learn this lesson too.) The fact that you've picked up this book only proves it. This book is about improving your writing craft. Only a writer would care about this. If you're reading it, you must care. You must be a writer.

In the pages that follow you'll find encouraging essays from novelists, short story writers, editors, creative nonfiction writers, publishers, children's book authors, a cartoonist, and even a literary agent (who is also a writer). Every one of these people had to own the moniker "writer" at some point or another. For many writers, this is not as easy as it sounds. But I think you'll find a group of kindred spirits in these essays—other writers who have learned a few things and who want to encourage you along on your journey.

Maybe you already write a blog post every day. Maybe you already have multiple books to your name. Or maybe you're like I was, just getting started and a little embarrassed of what feel like meager accomplishments. Whoever you are, if you write, then this book is for you.

You *are* a writer.

# I

# THE WRITING LIFE

# How to Use Math, Science, and the Power of Commitment—and Personal Vendettas—to Move Your Writing Forward

*By Alison Hodgson*

I don't want to write this chapter.

I'm sorry to have to tell you this—it's nothing personal—it's just that lately, I've been feeling the tiniest bit stuck, and on the best days I don't always like to write.

For the longest time I thought I had a fundamental flaw, being a writer who doesn't really enjoy writing, until I came across a quote by English playwright and novelist Dodie Smith who is most famous for the novel, then play, and eventual movie, *The One Hundred and One Dalmatians*. Smith began writing plays in the 1930s and was an almost immediate success. After the Second World War she began her first novel, *I Capture the Castle*. It took her three years to complete.

Smith wrote: "I write with great misery but am even more miserable when not writing—though I do enjoy thinking about writing and thinking about having written; it is the time in between that gets me down."

I about cried when I read that. I had never had anyone express so exactly, or honestly, my conflicted feelings about writing.

Here's the thing I have since learned: no matter your level of experience—whether you're just starting out or embarking on your hundredth book—for most writers, writing is a lot of hard work.

You may not call yourself a writer because you haven't been formally published, but writing is an integral part of who you are. In school you got straight-As on your stories and essays and whenever the teacher read student work to the class, your friends clamored for your stories. They *clamored*. You entered contests and won ribbons and awards but once you left school, you kind of got out of the habit, but now you're ready to get serious. You have this idea for a book. Let's says it's based on the true story of how your great, great, great grandmother fled Ireland during the potato famine and met your great, great, great grandfather on the ship coming over to the United States, and eventually married and settled outside Boston, and had a huge family, opened a brewery and became an American Success Story. It could be the next "Great American Novel," or really it could be nonfiction, maybe even a sort of memoir (you're not exactly sure about that) but you know it will almost certainly be a bestseller, and that it will practically write itself.

Oh dear.

So you get started, but you realize right away you need to do research first. Of course! Family stories can only take you so far; you have to soak in the atmosphere, get all the historical details just right.

And while you're at it, maybe you should explore the publishing business. You know your novel/memoir—your *epic*—is sure to be a hit, so there's no time like the present to calculate how soon you can quit your job and whether you're going to be able to buy ocean-side property or just lakefront.

Oh dear. Oh *dear*.

Maybe you know all about the publishing game. You learned long ago a platform isn't just a tiny stage, and if you're going to get published, you better build one. You have to start a blog. Ugh! Even the name is ugly, but you know you have to do it. So you set up your website and now you're just trying to write a stinking post so you can get to the real meat of your transcendent-sweeping-gonna-be-a-blockbuster...whatever-sort-of book TBD...whenever you finally get around to writing it.

Or maybe, if you're being perfectly honest, you're feeling a little stuck too. Well, you've come to the right place.

When I first got serious about writing I didn't even have an idea. Okay, I actually had tons of them, but no clear beginning. What I did have was three little kids I was educating at home and a wonderful husband who had the bad habit of leaving the country for weeks at a time for work. I had every excuse in the world not to write, but not writing had become an ache, an almost physical pain. I knew I had to find a way to make writing a part of my daily life and if I didn't, I would always regret it. But I had no clue where to start.

Commitment is a powerful thing. You don't have to know how you're going to do something to decide to do it. Have you made a commitment to write? If you haven't already, do it right now. We'll figure out the details later.

Ironically, teaching my children motion was what helped get me going. When we studied inertia I realized, despite acing high-school physics, I didn't really understand it. I thought it was synonymous with motionless. While it can mean that, Newton's first law of motion states that "an object at rest stays at rest and an object in motion stays in motion with the same speed and in the same direction unless acted upon by an unbalanced force."[1] In other words, objects tend to "keep on doing what they're doing." In fact, it is the natural tendency of objects to resist changes in their state of motion. This tendency to resist changes in their state of motion is described as inertia.

This was my "aha!" moment. Suddenly it was so clear: once I got going, I could "get stuck" writing as easily as I was stuck not writing. This changed everything for me. Sure, it could take a little extra effort to start moving, but being stuck wasn't a terminal condition and once I started moving, *momentum* was the force that would keep me going. I felt such hope. Short story: I knew I simply needed to begin writing. And so I did.

I didn't worry about word count or any big goals like writing a book or getting published. I didn't specify what days to write, or what time. I just wrote as much as I could between all my other responsibilities, day after day, story after story.

**Make a Ridiculously Achievable Writing Goal**

Back then all I worried about was writing as much as I could. After years and years of not writing, it was such a relief, quickly becoming a joy, to actually write, and that was all the momentum I needed then. For most of us, specific goals are critical for actually getting something written.

If you're feeling stuck, I encourage you to make a ridiculously achievable goal. Common advice is to shoot for 1,000 words a day, five days a week. That's great if you're already in the practice of regular writing but it may be daunting for a beginner. Would you tell a morbidly obese person on Day 1 of trying to get in shape to go run a marathon? Of course not. With exercise, most of us know, it's better to start small, and build up strength and stamina. It's the same with writing.

---

1 *http://www.physicsclassroom.com/Class/newtlaws/u2l1a.cfm#first*

A friend who wrote two novels, and was feeling stuck before her third, made the commitment to write 350 words a day, Monday through Saturday. Another friend who has written hundreds of nonfiction articles is tackling her first novel, while working full time and also facing some significant health problems. She made the commitment to write 100 words a day, Monday through Friday. Guess what? After just a few days in, both of them frequently surpassed their daily goals, and months down the road, they're both still consistently writing.

**Give Yourself an Assignment**

So you made your commitment to write; you set your ridiculously achievable goal, now it's time to give yourself an assignment. In other words, every night decide what "story" you're going to tell the next day. This is especially important if you have a big goal in the works, like a long article or even a book. Every big story (or article or essay) can be broken down into many smaller stories. All you need is a beginning, middle, and an end. As the inimitable Anne Lamott says, "Bird by bird." You break it down. You divide your bigger story (math!) into many, smaller stories, and one-by-one, you write them. Giving yourself assignments is a trick to help you ignore the empty page, and once you get going, to keep up your momentum.

Make a list of all the little stories or scenes within the larger story, and knock them off one-by-one. Take your book about your great, great, great grandparents and the Irish diaspora; there are so many places to begin. What about their courtship? That's actually a big story. How did they meet? You know it was shipboard, but who noticed the other one first? What small story is burning your fingers? What are you most eager to tell? That's where you start.

Don't worry if you don't know the whole story or if your writing isn't as good as you thought it would be—it almost certainly isn't—but take heart, it probably isn't as bad as you think, either. Keep writing. You can reread and edit later, and you'll figure out the bigger story as you write.

What if you don't have a big project in mind, or even a specific idea or goal? Make a list of stories you love to tell but have never written. Like that time your two-year-old locked you and your husband out of the house. Maybe you start with the moment of shock when you discovered your husband in the back yard with you but *without your baby*. (What was he thinking?!) Or maybe it's the flat-out horror you felt when you turned the handle and found the backdoor locked. Write it, moment after moment, scene by scene, until you have told the whole story, and then write another, and another, and another.

Some days will be a breeze and others a total slog. Some days you'll whip out hundreds of words, and others you'll struggle to string together ten. So it goes. Just keep going.

Don't worry if you get stuck—you almost certainly will. Just start all over: make a new commitment, set a ridiculously achievable goal, and give yourself a tiny assignment. Before you know it, you'll be moving forward again.

**But What About the Vendettas?**

So you get in the habit of writing. Take that little story about your toddler. You write it all: how you tried to talk to your son through the back door then raced to the kitchen window and clawed at it, tearing the wire screen with your bare hands while calling for your boy who came and stood in front of the sink and held his arms up to you sobbing; how you were ready to break the glass with your fists, but your boy was too close, so you tried (and failed!) to stay calm, you kept talking to him, choking back your own sobs, while your husband jimmied a living room window open, and got into the house and how you pulled your boy to you, and fell into your husband's arms after they met you at the front door and opened it together. You write it all and you realize it's not just a funny anecdote, it's grown into an essay about more than your little family (the best stories are always bigger than us). It's about the coexisting and competing frailties and strengths of parents. It's about failing one another and despite that, choosing each other again and again. It's about forgiveness and love.

You think it's good, maybe the best thing you've written, so you look through *Writer's Digest* and pick a few places, and you screw up the courage to send it to the first on your list, and you wait, and wait, and wait, and finally you get an email back and you're so excited until you read a terse response that boils down to "No, thank you." It's like a shot to your heart but you breathe in and out, and tell yourself that's just one, and you have a whole list, so you send it to the next one, and the next, and the next, and the next, and while the response time varies, it's always the same: NO.

"Rejection is part of the process" everyone tells you, and that's fine in the abstract, but in the concrete and terrible moments of actual no's that land like body blows, it's hard to be blasé and you wonder if this writing thing was such a good idea. What if all these rejections are more than just the process? Maybe you're no good...

Stop right there! Now is the time for vendettas. Perhaps you've never tried one and are feeling too downtrodden to learn. I have you covered. All you need to do is make my tried and true "You'll Rue the Day" list.

In ten years of pitching agents and editors, and working on several book ideas before landing a book contract, I racked up my own share of rejections. In the beginning I tried to be mature and dignified, "Well, I'm just glad I'm writing and sending things out. Getting rejections means I'm in the game." And while that was true, it didn't really help.

Once I sent a proposal to an agent per her request. I waited the appropriate amount of time, and then some, weeks turning into months, before "checking in" and then I waited some more, and finally she emailed to say she needed to pass on the project and—let's face it—me.

It was just another cruddy thing in a whole slew of terrible things going on in my life. I had every reason to despair, but something in my spirit rose up and I decided that agent would regret the day she turned me down, and just like that my "You'll Rue the Day" list was born.

Now before I go any further, it's important to understand the long, hard hours almost all editors and agents work. They deal with hundreds, even thousands, of submissions, which is just one part of their job, so they have to get through them as efficiently as possible—although every editor or agent I know feels like they're always running behind. Once they decide it's a no, they move on, and you need to as well.

Here's what you do: whenever you get any sort of rejection, stand up straight, hold your head high, lift your fist to the sky, and shake it while saying, as dramatically as you can muster (think of a soap-opera villain) "You'll rue the day you rejected my________!" Fill in the blank: essay, story, post, screenplay, manuscript, whatever!

I know this sounds like I'm a proponent of bitterness. I'm actually a champion of not giving up. I want you to keep writing, and the truth is moving forward in the face of rejection, after rejection, is hard. It's so easy to succumb to discouragement. When you threaten someone will rue the day they rejected you—and just to be clear here, you don't *actually* threaten anyone—you are recommitting to writing and to yourself as a writer, because the only way anyone (other than you) is going to rue to anything is if you get back in the chair and keep writing.

# Making Time to Write
## *By Amelia Rhodes*

Have you ever sat down to write and then found yourself rummaging through the fridge or fighting the urge to organize your closets or realizing you entered a time warp and somehow lost an hour of precious writing time to answering e-mails or updating social media?

In the early pages of *The War of Art*,[2] Steven Pressfield says: "There's a secret real writers know that wanna-be writers don't: And the secret is this, it's not the writing part that's hard. What's hard is sitting down to write."

Whether it's simply finding time in an already busy schedule, or gaining ability to make yourself sit and stay focused, we all face this battle of making time to write and making the most of our writing time.

I wrote my second book in thel midst of a life-changing move for my family, tucked away in the corner of a tiny rental home, surrounded by moving boxes, at Christmastime. It was the perfect time of year to move, adjust kids to a new home and routine, and meet a book deadline. (No it wasn't. Really, don't ever try that.)

By the grace of God, and with a whole lot of coffee, I made my deadline.

Most likely, you are a writer who also has a job to pay the bills and maybe a family that needs shuttled to activities, help with homework, and who insist on eating three times. Every. Single. Day. Your days start early, and you race from one responsibility to the next. Sometimes, you don't even get to sleep straight through the night thanks to kids. Or puppies. (Also of note, don't buy two puppies at the same time if you value sleep or uninterrupted writing time.)

When I wrote my first book, I was a stay-at-home mom with one child in elementary school and the other in kindergarten two-and-a-half days a week. I spent the days my youngest was in kindergarten at a local coffee shop, writing for six hours straight. I even had "my table and chair" that I

---

2 Pressfield, Steven. *The War of Art: Break Through Blocks and Win Your Inner Creative Battles*, Black Irish Entertainment LLC, 2012.

am convinced made me twice as productive. I turned in the manuscript two weeks ahead of my deadline without much stress.

By the time my second book deadline came around, both children were in school full time, but I was working four days a week at a local nonprofit. Thanks to the first book, I was also speaking regularly. At first, I tried to write every day. I'd snatch a paragraph here and there in between work and helping kids with homework and dinner and bedtimes. By the time I sat down to do serious writing on my day off, the ideas wouldn't flow. I had expended so much energy during the week. I felt so frustrated and guilty about what I wasn't getting done that my creativity suffered when I finally did have time to write. After I gave myself permission to do the bulk of writing on my day off, and stopped attempting much during the week, my productivity skyrocketed.

You're not alone in your struggle to make time to write. You can write in the midst of the chaos of your life. It might take creativity and a whole lot of coffee, but it can be done.

Here are four principles I have put into practice over the years, during various chaotic seasons, to make time to write.

**Find "Your" Time**

We each have times of the day where we are at our prime. My brain doesn't function well before 9 a.m. Just ask my family or anyone who has traveled with me to a writing conference.

If you are not a morning person, it's ok. You can still be a writer. However, it's likely that to add writing to a life already filled with responsibilities, you might need to start the day earlier, but you don't have to use that time to write.

I've found my morning and evening routines make or break my writing—even though they have nothing to do with writing. When I start the morning with plenty of time to get in a bit of exercise, some reading, and maybe even a load of laundry before the kids wake, the whole morning is less stressful, and I have more energy and creativity throughout the day. When I finish the day with a picked-up house (notice I didn't say clean), more reading, and setting out clothes for the next day, I find I've jumpstarted the next day, rather than waking and feeling like I'm already behind.

You may not have kids at home like I do, but we all have non-writing priorities that fill our days. What tasks can you get out of the way early in the day to open up time and creative energy later, when you're at your "prime" to write? Work with the way you are wired!

Find the prime writing time when your brain is most alive, and if at all possible write during that time of day. For me, it's after I've lived a full day and I have had time to let stories roll around in my head. I often write in the evening after my kids have gone to bed, or squeeze writing minutes in the afternoon while kids play or do homework. I almost never write first thing in the morning and absolutely not before at least one cup of coffee.

Figure out your writing prime time, and work with the way you're wired, not against it.

**Protect Your Time**

J.K. Rowling once talked about the importance of protecting her writing time: "Be ruthless about protecting your writing days. Do not cave to the endless requests to have 'essential' and 'long overdue' meetings on those days. The funny thing is that, although writing has been my actual job for several years now, I still seem to have to fight for time in which to do it. Some people do not seem to grasp that I still have to sit down in peace and write the books, apparently believing that they pop up like mushrooms without my connivance. I must therefore guard the time allotted to writing as a Hungarian Horntail guards its firstborn egg."[3]

If J.K. Rowling has to protect her time, how much more so must we who are still working jobs to pay the bills!

Once you've figured out your prime time, get creative in figuring out how you can set that time aside. Maybe it's taking a lunch break at work every day and sitting in your car or at your desk and writing for an hour. Maybe it's getting up earlier, maybe it's taking care of dinner prep or going to the gym at a different time. Whatever it is that you've managed to juggle–protect that time.

Block that time on your calendar. Even if it's just 30 minutes over lunch several times a week, set an appointment on your calendar with yourself, and don't break it. When someone asks if you're available for something, look at your calendar and say, "I'm sorry. I have an appointment at that time."

Everything and everyone will try to come between you and your writing. When I went back to college as a working adult, the school counselor

3 Rowling, J.K. https://www.goodreads.com/quotes/163742-be-ruthless-about-protecting-writing-days-i-e-do-not-cave

advised, "You will have to give up some things. You will need to explain to family and friends that no, you can't come to this gathering, or help with that party, because you are in school. You will have to make sacrifices. The people in your life need to understand that and respect it."

I once faced a big writing deadline shortly after my kids' spring break. I needed the week of spring break to make major progress on my project, yet I wanted to spend meaningful time with my kids. My mom offered a wonderful solution. We stayed at her place during spring break. I spent the days writing at a nearby coffee shop while she and the kids had grand adventures and made memories. I joined the fun in the evenings after a full day of writing. It was a win-win! Having family and friends who understand your writing priorities and can help you achieve your goals is priceless.

You are a writer. You need to protect your writing time. If you don't treat your writing time seriously, neither will those who surround you. Even if you haven't gotten paid yet for a single word, or you aren't making enough to live on, and apparently even if you are making millions of dollars, people will still not understand this. You have to be up-front and honest about protecting your time.

**Maximize Your Time**

For the past two years, Fridays have been my favorite day of the week. Fridays are my day off work, and I have exactly six and a half hours to myself while the kids are at school.

When my Friday routine began two years ago, as soon as the school bus pulled away from the house, I rushed to my computer at the kitchen table, or jumped in the car and sped to the nearest coffee shop. I clicked "new document" and stared at the white space of possibility with stories ready to be told. Six glorious hours! Visions of thousands of words danced in my head. Now, what were the stories again? The curser would often taunt me. "Nah, you've got nothin. You're a fraud."

All the brilliant ideas I had thought about during the week vanished like fog burned away by the sun. Panic set in as precious minutes ticked away and my word count sat at zero.

Today is another Friday, and I'm two hours into my writing session and cranking out the words. The first thing I did was open my to-do list, not a fresh document. Twelve items, listed in priority, with notes attached, direct my work today. (I use the list app, Wunderlist. It syncs with my phone and computer, and I can create multiple lists for different projects.) This essay was second on today's list, and I'm fleshing out paragraphs that were incomplete sentences and basic ideas I scratched out earlier this week. I know I won't finish all twelve items today, but next time I sit down to write, I'll know where to start.

What made the difference in productivity for my writing days? I learned that what I do before I sit down to write is crucial to maximizing my writing time.

Popular essayist and blogger, Shauna Niequist, calls this *stocking the pond:* "I'm talking about taking responsibility for stocking the pond of your own mind and heart, so that when it's time to tell a story, it's rich with details and life and texture, and so that when you're staring at a blank page, sure that you have nothing to say, all you have to do is walk out to the pond you've been stocking every day: fish upon fish upon fish.

"The first step in writing happens way before the typing: it's the stocking of the pond. Take notes on your phone, snap pictures, scribble on the back of receipts—notice everything. The first part of writing is noticing."[4]

This is something you can do every single day, whether or not you get minutes in front of your computer screen. During the most insanely busy seasons of life, I live by one rule: Do something for your writing life every day, even if you don't get a chance to sit down to write.

I've been known to freak out my passengers when driving by yelling, "Hey, Siri!"

The supposed "intelligent" assistant on my phone will answer, "Yes, Your Highness," or "Yes, Fart," depending on which child last had my phone and changed my name in the settings.

I'll order her first to change my name (again), and then to take a new note. I'll dictate random thoughts or an entire blog post while driving. Siri could seriously use a spelling upgrade, but I can usually make enough sense of her jumbled mess to jog my memory for what I was really trying to say.

I also always have a book available for research—whether it's a book loaded into the Kindle app on my phone, an audible book downloaded to my phone, or a physical book I carry in my bag. Whenever I'm surprised with a few spare moments, I can move my writing projects forward.

Find a tool or two that work for you to keep track of your prep work. I've found the Day One app to be helpful because you can tag entries, even

---

4 Niequist, Shauna, "Stocking the Pond," http://www.shaunaniequist.com/stocking-pond, Accessed January 13, 2015.

capture the weather, and attach a photo. Some writers email themselves. Try the notes app built into your smartphone. Keep a small journal and pen in your car, by the bed, or in your bag. Find something to capture the endless flow of ideas surrounding you every day.

**Squeeze in Extra Time**

Cracks and Canyons.

Every June, a group of writer friends and I share the cost of a weekend rental along Lake Michigan. We have just a few ground rules: the weekend is for writing or studying. If someone is working or reading, don't disturb her. We spread ourselves throughout the property. A number of us multitask by soaking up rare Michigan sun while typing out chapters. We socialize over shared meals, and in the evenings we might head into a nearby town. The house is eerily quiet for eight women, with the only sounds being the lake's lapping water and the clicking of keyboards. We treasure the time, and each year we celebrate the progress we've each made since the previous year's gathering.

Canyons of time are the big, open blocks of time, like our weekend lake retreat, when you can go deep in your writing and focus for a longer period. Get these whenever you can. Maybe you schedule one day a week where you have a couple hours or more—maybe on a Saturday morning or a Sunday afternoon. Get a Grand Canyon now and then too, where maybe once a month you spend an entire Saturday at your favorite coffee shop or once a quarter you get a hotel room off a discounted travel site and lock yourself away for a weekend.

You may not need to leave home for a writing retreat. When my friend Brenda is working to meet a deadline, she will "move into" her spare bedroom for a weekend. She instructs her husband and teenage son that she's not available and they need to fend for themselves. She treats the weekend as if she truly was away—not answering the phone or going to church. She stocks her guest room with her favorite drinks and snacks and spends the weekend writing, with even sleep and showers being optional. (Not showering is one way to make sure the family leaves you alone!) No spare bedroom? No problem! When Brenda's three older children were still at home, she bought a privacy screen, claimed a corner of a room, and still treated her time as a weekend "away" with the same rules.

Much of your writing may happen in the cracks of life. If you are paying attention, being intentional, and are prepared, you can get a lot of writing done in life's cracks.

I outlined 90 percent of my book *Pray A to Z: A Practical Guide to Pray for Your Community* while sitting in the dentist's waiting room during my kids' appointments. I needed to come up with 150 prayer topics, and with the backdrop of buzzing drills and kids crying, I found a lot of things to pray about.

When you have a spare moment, how do you spend it? It's tempting to sit down with the latest Buzzfeed quiz. (British actress Maggie Smith should be my grandmother, in case you were curious.) You could do laundry, catch up on e-mails, scroll social media, or you could write.

Whenever you have extra time, use it for writing. Write in the cracks—whether it's scripting a paragraph or a whole page, reading an article for research, posting a question on social media to get feedback on an idea, or scribbling a list of ideas for blog posts or articles. If you have five minutes—you can do something productive to move your writing forward. If you've stocked your pond and planned your work, you'll be ready to snatch every sliver of time you get.

Schedule canyons of time every week if you can, even if they're small spaces of time. But when you are surprised with an extra few minutes of time between appointments or a child takes a longer than usual nap (we can all dream, right?), use it to write.

You can do this. I believe in you. I can't wait to see what you create.

15 minutes a day! ?

- Making Writing a priority / Copying good stuff

- Make a ridiculous easy project to do

- journaling...

Accountable?

"Chap book"?

# Blogging Basics: How a Blog Can Further Your Writing Career

*By Robert G. Evenhouse*

If you ever find yourself in a room full of writers, and if you are feeling a little devious, simply interject the words "platform", "social media", or "online presence" into the conversation and wait for their reactions. For writers, social media can play many roles: an obstacle, a gateway, or a frustrating combination of both.

I have a wife, four kids, and a full-time job. Writing gets tucked in the cracks of my busy schedule. Social media gets even less of my attention. But when I came across a blog post by Chad Allen, the editorial director of Baker Books, I started to reconsider the purpose of blogging. The beginning of Allen's blog post went like this:

*I've been doing something for years and just now noticed it. Whenever a book proposal crosses my desk, I Google the author's name. If I cannot find them in the first few search results, I move on.*[5]

I was upset when I first read this. I barely have time to write. How can I cultivate an online presence as well? I want to be a writer, not a blogger or marketer. The following paragraphs address this very problem.

Before we delve into the why or why not of social media, we need to address the first question every writer should ask: Why do I write? Knowing the answer to this question can save a lot of frustration and help solve the anxiety of whether a blog or website is essential or not.

## One Question Every Writer Should Ask

*Why do you write?* Is it to share a fun story? To create a self-published work? Do you want to be published traditionally someday? Do you want to write for a living? What is your goal? After you have taken some time to ponder this question we can address the role of social media in your

5 http://www.chadrallen.com/2015/08/27/google/

writing life. I encourage you to write down the answer to this question and post it somewhere you will see it every day. Use it as your guide. Refer back to it when you feel lost or overwhelmed.

If your goal is to be published, then we need to reconsider the quote from Allen. If an editor's first reaction to a manuscript landing on his desk is to Google the author's name, then social media is something writers should carefully consider.

The thought of managing an online presence while balancing your marriage, kids, day job, time with friends, let alone your writing project, can be overwhelming. I understand. I live that busy life. But what if maintaining a blog could become less an object in the way, and more a tool to use to your advantage?

Have you heard of Joanna Gaines from the HGTV show *Fixer Upper*? She wrote a blog that was instrumental in her landing her TV show and recent book.[6] Jeff Goins and Jon Acuff were both bloggers before they became full-time writers and entrepreneurs. *The Martian* was a serialized novel released in chapters, created as a file to share with friends before Andy Weir landed a publishing deal and later a movie contract.[7]

These stories are the exception, not a formula to be followed, but the fact remains that having work posted somewhere on the Web creates an opportunity for someone to notice your work and connect with you. Josh Mosey, who is in my writers' group, The Weaklings, was contacted by *The Wall Street Journal* about his post on the connection between having a messy workspace and creativity.[8] They wanted his thoughts for an article.

Still unconvinced? Consider this. If you are a hiring manager looking to fill a particular position, would you search for an individual with no experience? You would likely want someone with several years of experience. The same can be said for publishers. Publishers want to build a catalog of great books, but they also need to keep the lights on. If they had to choose between two similar authors, one of whom has a blog with regular readers and one who does not, which author do you think they will choose?

The tension may be rising in your chest. You feel the pressure. However, let's approach this from a different perspective.

---

6 Chip and Joanna Gaines, *The Magnolia Story* (Nashville, Tennessee: W Publishing, an Imprint of Thomas Nelson, 2016).

7 http://www.businessinsider.com/how-andy-weirs-the-martian-became-so-successful-2015-6

8 https://joshmosey.wordpress.com/2014/04/17/my-messy-desk-under-fire/

Have you ever played the game *Contra* on the original Nintendo? There are only six buttons to work with, three lives, and no Save Point. You must finish it in one sitting or lose all of your progress. It's nearly impossible to defeat the entire game. But then the internet happened, and soon after, cheat codes were born.

Using the proper cheat code on *Contra* can grant you unlimited lives and an easy win after a few hours. This is what a blog can be: a publishing cheat code. What if you try all you can to polish your manuscript, but you also have an online presence, with active followers who are tuned into your work? This does not guarantee that you'll be published, but it does make you less of a risk for a publisher and therefore a little more difficult to pass up. There are countless stories of editors finding writers through their websites.

**So, Where Do I Start?**

If you only read the paragraph in the previous section about successful bloggers who landed book contracts, then you might think blogging is a simple process. But the terrifying reality is that you are practicing the craft of writing in public and people can see your typos. Thousands of blogs are created each day and competition for attention is fierce. It can be intimidating to both share your work and worry about how to do it right.

If you've made the decision to start a blog or website, your work has only just begun. Now is the best time to start. Ten years ago you had to become a computer programmer or pay a lot of money to have a website created. Then you had to pay to host your own site. If you developed your own website you would likely spend most of your time in development and only a fraction of it actually writing. Today you don't have to be technically savvy to create a blog. You can create one for free, and in less than one hour. Then you can start writing.

The main choice you have to make is between creating a self-hosted website, or creating a site hosted by Blogger, Wordpress.com, Weebly, or another blogging application. Many providers can host your blog and the choices can be overwhelming. I recommend starting out with a wordpress.com site. Why? It's free, easy to set up, and no programming is required. It is also used by most bloggers, powering 24 percent of internet pages, and therefore easier to connect with other writers and begin to form an audience. Simply drop in a theme, add an about page, an e-mail widget so your audience can subscribe to your blog, and begin your first post.

There are millions of little tweaks you can make to create the perfect blog. If you are like me (easily distracted and frozen by indecision) I recommend following the steps in the paragraph above. Theme, about page, e-mail widget, and post. It can be easy to try to get it perfect, but don't worry about that at first. You will probably get bored with the theme you choose and will want to create a different look. Later, you may invest in a professional logo and add a different header. However you dress up your blog, the point is to create a space where you can be found and your audience can connect with you.

**Elements of Blogging**

Writing is an arduous road. Blogging is no different. The ability to create fresh content can leave you exhausted with nothing to give your book. To ensure you stay on track I have developed a simple system to help construct posts faster and not leave you empty when it comes time to write.

Step One is the creation phase. I start out with a paragraph or a one-sentence thought or quote that has made an impact on me. I usually keep these ideas in a small pocket-sized journal, a folder in my Gmail account, or the notes application on my phone—whatever I have handy at the moment. This helps me compile a collection of ideas. I try to remember what inspired me and made me consider it a potential blog post. This step takes less than a minute to do and I can do it almost anywhere.

Step Two is the development phase. This step requires me to explore the idea. I begin with a question or challenging statement about my idea, just like the hook of a chapter in a book. This question is one I hope my readers are asking as well. After that I do my best to create three to five paragraphs about the question, and then finish with an answer. I do not edit here. Editing my work while the idea is taking shape is a sure way to stamp out the fire of productivity.

The final step is the most important. This is where I begin to critique my work. I cut it down to a certain number of words, which is usually 300 or fewer. I revise the paragraphs and make sure my blog answers the question or statement that started the post.

These are my three steps. This process works for me. You might need something else to keep you working. The most important part of creating blog posts is developing a system that works for you so blogging is not a chore, but a writing exercise.

Creating blog posts on your site can be tedious. Like any writing activity, there are no set rules, and therefore endless ways to package your content or fret over how to use each and every word. Publishers are watching, right? This means writer's block can surface often unless you have a plan to combat it.

Below are the key components of my posts. They don't need to be in this order, but I try to recall them as I put the content together. I call it my blog recipe. I stole that line and some of these bullet points from Michael Hyatt.[9]

*Explanatory title with SEO keywords.* Search engine optimization keywords are words and phrases that help people find your website when they use search engines. This is often the last thing I do.

*Solid opening paragraph.* I spend most of my word-worrying here.

*Perfect Image.*

*Relative Story.* This is personal, a story or blog I read. It connects me to my audience.

*Links to other sites that relate to my post.*

*Tags.* These allow my readers to click and see other posts with the same topics.

*Schedule the post for the correct day and date.*

*Action step or closing question.*

Having a list, or recipe, to refer back to can help you stay on track and continue to move forward. The best and worst thing about blogging is that there is no wrong way to do it. Remember, if a process doesn't work for you, create one that does.

**This is Your Laboratory**

Austin Kleon is one of my favorite writers. He calls himself a writer who draws. If you've ever read *Show Your Work!* or *Steal Like An Artist,* you will know why. He takes the pressure off of himself as a writer to point you toward interesting work. He calls himself a connector. This may seem counter-intuitive, pointing your readers to other work, but this is how he's chosen to use his "laboratory" on the internet. Its creative and works for him, two essential ingredients we bloggers need.

---

9 Michael Hyatt, *Platform: Get Noticed in a Noisy World* Thomas Nelson, 2012, pp.83-84, see also www.michaelhyatt.com/recipe.html

If you are unsure of what to write about, remember: this is *your laboratory*. Make it fun, inventive, but cohesive. Keep to a common theme so you always have something to write about. I suggest writing content surrounding one of these three themes.

One: *You have an interesting collection of ideas to share*. For example, you share what you read, or listened to, and point your audience toward that work. You found an interesting video of Neil Gaiman on YouTube that poignantly describes the writing experience and want you others to find it too. You read the essay collection *Scratch*, about writers making money, and want to promote it because it was helpful to you. The posts are not about you but about things you find interesting and helpful in your writing journey.

Two: *You are an expert*. The quote from the editor at the beginning of this essay carries weight. He is on the inside, been down the publishing road before, and can provide the inside scoop. As an expert, people will come to you because you have expertise in a certain field and want to learn from what you have to say.

Three: *You are sharing in your journey*. This is not an online journal *per se*, but instead you share your day-to-day struggle of your life and publishing dreams. I once wrote about the time I built a new writing desk and how the very next day my daughter wrote on it with permanent marker! Then later that evening she showed me the book she'd written and illustrated in the same space I write my own. Maybe you'll unload a rant about how some stupid author convinced you to start a ridiculous blog in the first place. Whatever the topic is, it surrounds the idea of the writer's struggle. It is different from a journal because you are not sharing your darkest secrets or drama about your day job, but rather the latest research you read about a topic you regularly blog about.

These are the three types of blogs that tend to keep my attention. Occasionally, the journey sharer, like author-blogger Jon Acuff was in his early days, becomes the expert. But otherwise the posts are connected under one central idea.

One last recommendation I have is for fiction writers. If you are writing short stories or consider releasing chapters of fiction online, I suggest not posting them on your blog. Why? Because if you want to publish traditionally, publishers often want exclusive rights to your piece and if you have posted them on your blog that violates the agreement. If you are unsure, return to the portion earlier in this chapter about the one question every writer should ask. That will provide clarity for you in this matter. For some writers it may be the right decision to publish your fiction online, but not for every writer.

**What to Do from Here**

Somerset Maugham is credited with saying, "There are three rules for writing. Only no one knows what they are."[10] Whether Maugham actually made that statement or not is unimportant. What is important is that you create a blog not because I told you to do so, but because you believe it is the best decision for your work.

Take what is helpful from this chapter and leave the rest. I hope it challenged, encouraged, and gave you inspiration to give blogging a chance. And, if you launch your blog, look for me on the web and let me know. Type *Robert Evenhouse* in the search bar and look for me in the top few search results.

---

10 http://www.thecreativepenn.com/2011/09/14/3-rules-for-writers/

# II

# HONING YOUR CRAFT

# Essays for Everyone: Telling the Stories that Shape Your life

*By Tom Springer*

I get why most people—including writers—may flinch at the thought of writing a creative essay. For one thing, the very word "creative" can sound pretentious and off-putting. Ever hear someone use the term creative poem, creative novel or creative magazine feature article? Probably not. It's pretty much implied that if you write any of these, it's already creative.

Then there's that musty, lecture-hall word "essay." It takes us back to essay questions on tests, to shotgun/spin-the-prayer-wheel answers that sought to obfuscate our shaky knowledge of a subject. Or worse, to college application essays, where we tried to make our 18-year-old rookie selves come across as incipient versions of Steve Jobs or Mother Teresa.

If that's been your experience, then it's time to learn what no teacher or college admissions office ever told you: that creative essays are a flexible, lively, and yes, infinitely creative form of literary art. An essay can give voice to your life's most meaningful stories. An essay can incorporate elements of journalistic reporting, fiction-like scene setting and poetic turns of phrase. An essay, with all its kitchen sink eclecticism, can also be a welcome alternative for writers who need a break from the structure of fiction or journalism.

For readers, there's something innate about a good essay that just feels right, the way that an old flannel shirt or eggs served sunny-side up in a small-town diner feels right. That's because essays follow the same natural, narrative flow that we use to share stories with friends and family. Consider this "tail" from my own life. While I haven't (yet) made it an essay, it does contain many elements of one.

It uses relevant facts: "At 2 a.m. our tom cat was yowling from that big maple on the corner."

It includes dramatic dialogue: "A cop showed up and said, 'Is that your cat?' and I said, 'Do I legally have to answer that?'"

It builds suspense, and offers cues—foreshadowing—of what's coming next: "Did I mention that Larry, who lives two doors down, is a Channel 3 cameraman?"

Then, it ends with an attempt to make sense of it all: "After my knucklehead cat appeared on the 11 o'clock news, I heard from people who haven't answered my Christmas cards in five years. How come a 15-second TV soundbite moved them to call, when our *hand-signed* family newsletter did not?"

Essays. You've been telling them your whole life. Why not jot them down and get paid for it?

**Where Essays Live**

Creative essays (although they're rarely called that) appear in magazines, newspapers and blogs, and as public radio commentaries. They're typically 500 to 1,500 words in length, although they can run 5,000-10,000 in high-end literary journals. Some of my favorite essays run on the back pages of magazines. The best of these are well-honed pieces that sparkle with evocative writing, cogent insights and delightful, I didn't-see-that-coming endings. Newspapers also publish essays of the wonkier variety on their opinion pages. These typically combine first-person knowledge with a call for action, such as a former football player turned lawyer who calls for new player guidelines to prevent head injuries.

Travel magazines prefer first-person pieces, because for arm-chair travelers, they capture the hardships and epiphanies that makes trips to Istanbul, or Indiana, read like a personal quest for meaning. First-person columns on parenting or business topics also make for popular mini-essays. A writer can combine examples from his or her life with useful technical knowledge in ways that make readers come back for more.

**The Power of "I"**

By now, you may be ready to stop reading an essay about essays and go write one of your own. But first, you should keep in mind a paradox of the trade. By that I mean the risks and rewards of using everyone's favorite pronoun: the "I."

I was trained in journalism and public relations, fields where writers are paid to tell other people's stories. You start with a story angle, gather facts and quotes from various sources, and write it up in third-person form. As in, "the mayor said today," or "the city councilman argues that . . ." There's no room for your own musings or opinions. A reporter or PR staffer could go their entire career and never once use the word "I" in a story.

Well, by the time I hit my late 30s, I'd had my fill of that. I'd already stifled my voice with 10 years of third-person writing. Plus, I'd served as speechwriter for the CEO of a major foundation. Cruel irony, that. I could finally use "I" in my writing—but as the mouthpiece for a 60-something corporate exec who was partial to shiny penny loafers.

My break came when I began a master's degree program in environmental journalism at Michigan State University. I had become enamored with *A Sand County Almanac,* a seminal collection of essays by Aldo Leopold, patron saint of modern ecology. For a master's project, I wrote six essays based on my experiences of rural life in southern Michigan.

But when I turned them in, my advisor said they weren't "personal enough." I hadn't used the "I" with enough depth of purpose to advance my themes. Later, I submitted the rewritten collection, expanded from six to 18, for publication as a book, *Looking for Hickories* (University of Michigan Press). The editor's reply was positive: she wanted to publish. But only if I would revise them—a second time! "I'm afraid," she said, "there's too much of 'you' in these stories."

Therein lies the first-person rub. Our life experiences give essays the realism that only first-person accounts can. Yet we have to find the right balance, because good essays aren't diaries. While first-person writing can be therapeutic, most readers don't want to read therapy or mentally paw through the underwear drawer of your life. Instead, your experiences should be a companionable guide, a bridge that leads readers to new discoveries. They may not know about sailing, playing the banjo, cheating at cards or fighting the Taliban. But your first-person self can take them there, if you ground your writing in universal themes such as love, faith, loss, birth, death and redemption.

To develop a deft ear for the first-person, you'll need to make yourself a student of the essay. For starters, find a copy of *The Best American Essays* series published annually by Houghton Mifflin Harcourt. Read them first for sheer enjoyment. Then the next time through, take note of the structure. How did the essay begin and end? How did the writer handle transitions from one section or scene to another? How do they use pacing and dialogue? Think of an essay like a river. It's not only the main current of the story that's interesting. It's also the little eddies, sometimes only two or three sentences long, where you can linger and provide perspective before easing back into the faster waters of the story.

Yet even with preparation, the hardest part is usually the beginning (OK, and sometimes the middle and the ending). So at the risk of sounding un-creative, let me offer four steps on how to shape and write a creative essay.

**Personal Experience**

The creative power that drives a good essay must come entirely from the writer. It's derived from deep experience, even if it's something we don't have, but have long yearned for: a real house, after too many years in a shoe-box apartment; a good night's sleep after months of insomnia. For me, the best essays are inspired by the deepest loves, fears and questions I have for the world.

The impetus for my essay "What's Right About the Night," came after an arsonist torched our 19th century, timber-frame barn on a frigid, January night. This ignorant act of vandalism prompted me to reflect on light and darkness.

First, there'd been the hellish flames themselves, bright and visible for miles around in our rural neighborhood. Then there was the darkness of the arsonist's heart. How could someone willfully destroy such a venerable piece of pioneer handiwork? At the same time, I've always enjoyed being outside in the dark. The old barn didn't have lights and I liked it that way. Why mar the restful darkness of a country night with a Death Star yard light that blots out the heavens with its glare? These contrasts, and the question of whether to install lights on the new barn, were woven through the story.

With personal experiences, it's important to remember that you don't need an A-to-Z catalog of all that happened. For example, if your Army infantry platoon went on 12 combat patrols in Iraq, you don't have to describe them all. Pick one that represents a typical mission. In the case of "What's Right About the Night," I'd already written a 10,000-word essay about the barn fire. My story here was about the merits of dark and light, a theme that deserved an essay of its own. To help frame the essay in my mind, I asked myself: "What value does darkness have in a 24/7, floodlit world?" Answering that helped me select aspects of my personal story that best supported the theme.

**Background Knowledge**

While your personal experience should shape and propel the essay, it's not the whole story. You still need a factual case to support the essay's larger theme. Here, you'll need to put on your research hat and be as rigorous and accurate as a journalist. For "What's Right About the Night," I needed to know more about the physical benefits of darkness. It wasn't enough that I liked it—my readers had to see its value, too.

To make my case, I mentioned how too much artificial light confuses birds, who crash into buildings; how salmon fry (minnows) prefer dark streams, where their prey can't find them; how newly-hatched sea turtles can become confused by lights, and crawl toward streets and parking lots instead of the ocean. I cited Centers for Disease Control research to show how sleeping in a room bathed by a streetlight's glow may contribute to hormone-related cancers.

Here, too, balance is crucial. No need for five or six examples when two or three will suffice. Too many dry details will bog down your essay's narrative flow. Also, use facts accurately, but phrase them in ways that reflect your own voice and pacing. You don't want the essay's factual sections to read as if you've lifted them verbatim from a newspaper. Because there's a word for that ... it's called plagiarism.

**Form and Sequence**

The good news about essays? They have no established form. The bad news? You guessed it: they have no established form. With an essay, you've got to create your own story blueprint. To find the right overall structure, look at your building blocks: the key scenes, factual elements and what aspects of these would make for a good beginning and ending.

Some essays open with an action sequence. That's how I began, "Local Man, 54, Kills First Turkey:"

*I didn't know that a 25-pound turkey could be so strong. But it seemed like this one had enough flap to carry us both airborne across the barnyard. Even with his wings held fast in a bear hug, I could scarcely contain his fury. His scaly, four-inch claws tore a foot-long gash in my sweatshirt. My main advantage was that I knew where we were going: to the steel funnel that dripped red from a fence post 75 feet away. It was harvest time, our knives were sharp, and the Thanksgiving reckoning was at hand.*

My brother and I had raised a dozen turkeys (he did the work, I only paid for the feed). I led with the butchering, since it was my only real involvement with the birds. I wanted to shake my readers from their complacency, just as killing my family's Thanksgiving turkey barehanded had shaken me from my complacency.

At other times, a summary explanation can set up the action sequence that follows. I did that for "The Best Wild Fruit You Never Tasted," which sings the praises of a little-known wild fruit call the serviceberry:

*There is perhaps no wild fruit that tastes as good as the serviceberry. When serviceberries ripen in June, it's tempting to gulp them down by the handful, grunting all the while like a happy caveman until the purple juice dribbles down your chin.*

A light-hearted opening worked best for this essay. It set up an action sequence that has me picking fruit from a serviceberry tree in the city. It's lunch time, I'm in a shirt and tie and several passersby assume I've either flipped my wig or aim to kill myself by ingesting poison fruit. Without ample set up, the humor of that scene wouldn't have made as much sense. That's why it's important to let your material dictate what sort of opening to use.

Another key factor to consider in your essay's structure is time sequence. Sometimes it's straight chronological: this happened, then that happened and so on. In other cases, you can use the classic *in media res* approach (Latin for "in the middle of things.") Here, you begin at a crucial point in the story and then circle your way back to it. For instance, imagine an 18-year-old girl who's about to meet her father for the first time. The writer could start with that scene, and backtrack to explain the trials she's faced as a fatherless daughter.

Since my essays cover nature, the four seasons provide a logical structure. Even with that, there's room for creativity. The finest example I've ever read would be Aldo Leopold's "Good Oak," in *A Sand County Almanac.* The book's chapters follow the months of the year. Yet in "Good Oak" Leopold does something simple, but extraordinary. In the essay, Leopold mans a crosscut hand saw to turn a fallen oak into firewood. As the saws cuts through the tree, he uses the rings on its trunk to comment on Wisconsin's environmental history. In 1865, the last elk was killed ... in 1907 Wisconsin parted with its last cougar and so on. It's a haunting way to chronicle the ruin and recovery of the state's natural resources.

**Wisdom Synthesis**

The end is near, and though we sophisticated readers hate to admit it, we prefer our stories wrapped up in a tidy bow. In other words, we expect them to end with meaning. As a writer, this is where you make sense, in a 2+2 = 5 way, of what your essay teaches the world. I call this wrap-up the Wisdom Synthesis. Whatever question inspired you to write the essay must be answered or at least guessed at here. And sorry, you can't fake this one either, though Lord knows I've tried. Push too hard and your Wisdom Synthesis will sound forced or corny. Leave it out and your essay's ending will fall flat. Yet while you can't rush it, have faith. The summing up often comes when I least expect it. Let your subconscious do its job while you do something else: run, garden, pray, brush your teeth, take a hot shower and your muse will eventually offer up a solution. When it does, write it down quick (pull off the road if need be!) before that just-right phrasing fades away. Until then, I'll leave you with ending of mine:

*I'll probably never understand why someone would burn down a beautiful old barn ... But I do know that what we see in the evening sky—whether it's the diamond twinkle of stars or the orange glare of suburbia—is a reflection of how we view the world. And we shouldn't allow the darkness that lies within a few human hearts to overcome what's good about the night.*

# Write the Truth: Vulnerability in Nonfiction Writing

*By Ellen Stumbo*

**Life is Unpredictable**

When I was pregnant with my second daughter, a routine ultrasound mid-pregnancy showed several markers consistent with Down syndrome. Rather than preparing myself for the birth of a child with a disability, I pretended it was all a bad dream because I didn't know how to handle the situation. We did not have a definite diagnosis, and I convinced myself I was too young to have a child with Down syndrome. As I pushed my daughter into this world, my midwife guided her out and lifted her to me. Even before she was in my arms I could tell from her physical characteristics she had Down syndrome.

This is where I wish I could tell you I hugged my baby and fell in love immediately. But I didn't. I was ignorant about disability and knew only the stereotypes associated with the condition. All I could see in my baby when I looked at her was Down syndrome. She was also born with two holes in her heart and an immature liver. I was grieving her diagnosis, and I wrongly believed I didn't want anything to do with this new life. In my mind, my baby was supposed to be healthy and "perfect." A child with a disability was not what I wanted.

I was also a pastor's wife at the time, and I felt I had an obligation to pretend I was fine with her diagnosis. I dished out Christian clichés to make other people feel better while inside I was shaking my fist at God. I also carried an immense amount of guilt for not being a love-struck mother over her new-born baby. *Someone is going to figure out how I'm really feeling. They are going to figure out I am so broken I seem unable to love my child. A mother is supposed to love unconditionally, what is wrong with me!*

As the days went by, I felt worse and worse about myself. I was convinced I was a failure as a mother, unable to look past the disability and therefore holding back love and affection for my child. I cried several times throughout the day and stopped going to church with the excuse my baby was sick. I was coming undone.

When my daughter was two weeks old her pediatrician suspected she had a serious liver condition. She was transferred to Mayo Clinic and we were told we would be there for a while. The second night we were there, one of the nurses encouraged my husband and I to get out for a little while.

My husband, Andy, decided we needed to go to a bookstore and buy any books we could find about Down syndrome. We made our way to the miniscule section on "Special Needs Parenting." I reached for a book about teaching motor skills to babies with Down syndrome, but my husband placed a hand on my shoulder and said, "I think this is the book you should read right now." He handed me a copy of the book, *Gifts: Mother's Reflect on How Children with Down Syndrome Enrich Their Lives.* The cover showed a picture of a baby with Down syndrome, I flipped to the back of the book and read, "Having a baby with Down syndrome is not something most parents would willingly choose." That one sentence was powerful enough to make me wipe a tear from my eye. Yes, that is how I felt. I would not have willingly chosen this life, and someone else understood. Someone else had felt it too. Then I read the rest of the back cover—I finally knew I wasn't alone.

Clutching the book tight against my chest I knelt down. I could have tried to hold back the tears, but I was at a place where holding back and pretending was becoming too hard. With just a few paragraphs from a book written by women who had walked in my shoes, I felt I did not have to pretend anymore. I wept in the middle of the parenting aisle at Barnes & Noble. *Someone else knows and understands how I feel.*

**The Most Personal is the Most Universal**

It is hard to let people see into the dark places. We live in a social-media culture where so much of what we show is the "pretty" and the "perfect." We want to believe we are people who achieve success, look the part, and reach for their goals. At least some of us do and we try to put on a good-looking front. Letting people see the messy and hard is not what we are naturally inclined to do. What will people think if they can see our shortcomings?

However, I believe there is much to be learned from our failures, from the messy, from the hard. The parts of our stories perhaps we wish we could keep hidden may be the very essence of what makes us relatable and real.

For those who have struggled to hold on, those who feel they might be coming undone, our raw and real stories might be exactly what they need to hear. Our stories might be what allows them to let go and begin a journey to find hope and healing.

Henri Nouwen says, "The most personal is the most universal, the most hidden is the most public, and the most solitary is the most communal. What we live in the most intimate places of our beings is not just for us but for all people. That is why our inner lives are lives for others."[11]

If you wrestle with something, chances are someone else does, too. If something unspeakable happened to you—as hard as it is to believe—there is probably someone else who has gone through a similar experience. Our unique stories are not as unique as we believe them to be, there are others who upon hearing them will say, "You, too? I thought I was the only one."

When I became serious about my writing, I knew I had to do for others what the women from the book *Gifts* had done for me. I wanted to reach out and let other people know they were not alone. Turns out it is hard to connect with someone who seems to be a hero, yet we find a connection with those who have wrestled like we do, those who have been in the pit, too. Those are the people we trust, because they understand what it is like to be us.

### Being Vulnerable Takes Courage

I wanted to offer hope and encouragement through my writing for any parent struggling with their child's diagnosis. And I knew in order to write like that, I had to be willing to let people see me as I really was—broken over my daughter's diagnosis, yet offering hope because I was now on the "other side." I was no longer ignorant about disability and I was able to see the beauty of my daughter's diagnosis. In order to share my new understanding, I needed to let people see the darkness that came before the light. But did I really want others to know my darkest thoughts during that period of time? Did I want them to see how broken I truly was? On the other hand, what if there was another mom who had just received a diagnosis of Down syndrome and was struggling the same way I did? Could I be brave for that mom? Did I have the courage to reach out and allow my words to speak to her heart and say, *you are not alone, these feelings are a natural process of becoming a parent of a child with a disability. You will find joy and love. You will dream again.*

---

11 *Bread for the Journey: A Daybook of Wisdom and Faith,* Henri J. Nouwen, San Francisco, HarperOne, 1997, 2:23

Writing with vulnerability requires compassion. First for yourself, as you learn to accept and love yourself for who you are. The good and the bad. Then compassion extends to others, because you understand the pain and the challenges they could be facing. Compassion understands your story can reach out to deep places with words that will make a difference in someone else's life.

It wasn't easy to write this way at first. I didn't want people to know how hard it was for me to accept my daughter's diagnosis. I feared what other people would think about me, but it especially forced me to be real with myself.

But I learned that writing with vulnerability means having the courage to take a closer look at our pain, hurt, shortcomings, failures or flaws. It can be a painful process, especially if we are not ready or able to find hope in the journey. In my experience, it is only when we have hope that we are able to write vulnerably. And it is only when we have hope that we can benefit those who read out words.

Vulnerability might be what allows people to connect with our writing and journey with us. If we found hope, perhaps they will, too. We need to be able to write: "This is me when I was in the pits. This is what I felt. This is how I lived. It was bad. Then I found help. It was hard to ask for help. This is what help did for me. This is I how I feel now. This is how I live now."

**Knowing What and When to Share**

Many of us who write nonfiction do so because we feel we have a story to share, something to teach or a message to spread. And these purposes are tightly connected to our life experiences. Perhaps we've learned an important life lesson we feel other people need to hear, too. We want to make a difference for those who stumble upon our writings.

I would venture to say most of us feel passionate about the topics we write about and we hope that after people read our words, they leave changed, challenged or encouraged.

Like many other writers do, I have a personal blog. This is where I write all sorts of stories and anecdotes that relate to parenting children with disabilities. It is not surprising that my most popular blog posts are those where the message is raw and real. These are the posts where people find connection. Because of vulnerability, people can see themselves in my messy and hard experiences. It is in these stories people recognize they are not alone.

I want my writing to be a safe space where people find *hope*.

Yet there is one thing we do need to talk about, because writing the truth doesn't mean we write without boundaries. We have to consider our readers, those we might write about and even ourselves.

Writing with vulnerability does not mean we share every detail. Some things are private and should stay that way. Some stories are too painful for others and it might not be time to share. Writing with vulnerability means we share responsibly.

If you are unsure about how much to share, you can ask yourself the following questions:

*What is the purpose of my sharing this detail or story?*

*Could this particular story hurt someone I love?*

*How would I feel if someone I love wrote this story about me?*

*If I am writing about someone I love, am I upholding their dignity and showing them respect?*

*If I am writing about someone living, do I have their permission to share?*

*If I am writing about someone else, am I attributing emotions or actions to them based on how I would feel? For example, am I interpreting silence as someone being angry when in reality I have no idea what that person was feeling?*

*If I was gone tomorrow, would I want this to be part of my legacy?*

*Are all the details I am sharing necessary to convey the message of my story?*

*Could this story potentially hurt someone else in the future?*

*In the future, could I regret sharing this story?* If I am unsure, it is best not to share.

*Could there be any legal implications if I share this story?* When in doubt, seek legal advice from a professional.

*Will someone reading feel encouraged, understood, or helped?*

*How does this story help someone else?* If it only helps me, this belongs in a private journal.

Even when we write the truth, we must seek to be reliable and trustworthy. There are many stories I could share, yet I know those stories could hurt people I care about. Perhaps someday I will share those, but I know this is not the time.

Because much of my writing centers on parenting children with disabilities, I walk a fine line between sharing my story versus sharing my children's stories. There are certain things I do not share because they would strip my children of their humanity. Their disabilities do not make them any less human, and while many parents could relate to some of our challenges, my children come first and some of those potentially relatable stories are not for the public. They are only for us. My children's dignity and respect take precedence over my writing.

**Why We Write the Truth**

It is a human trait to want connection. Yet, many people feel isolated, especially when they are wrestling with challenges in life. Isolation is hard. Isolation can lead to despair and hopelessness. We write the truth because we want to create a connection to those people who read our words. On a profound level, we let them know they are not alone.

It seems as if culture is filled with pretense nowadays—so much pretending. The Facebook posts of smiling people, photos that show happy marriages, happy children baking cookies, friends gathering and laughing. Sometimes those images and stories seem so different from our own broken marriages, our challenges in parenting or perhaps our lack of friends. People want to hear *real* stories. They want to connect with people who are like them, people who are not "perfect" and who stumble and fall through this complicated, unpredictable life.

Writing the truth allows people to see you, the real you. Not the you who puts on a front or who looks "perfect" on the outside. Vulnerability says, "This is the good, and this is the bad. This is me. All of me." No pretense, just real.

There was a time I wondered, "If someone can see what is inside, will they still like me?" But it is in the vulnerable moments that I have been able to connect with people most deeply.

If you were to google Down syndrome, you might find one of the characteristics is low muscle tone. I can tell you about it and share the clinical side of low muscle tone. But I can also tell you that because my daughter has low muscle tone, when she hugs me, it's like she melts into my arms—a heavy, comforting embrace that *grounds me*. Her hugs feel differently because of her low muscle tone, but they also feel full of love. This is what writing with vulnerability is like. It's sharing the human side of our experiences beyond what other people perceive.

We write the truth because we *have* to. Words are powerful. Words can offer hope and healing and connection with readers.

Write the truth.

# Visualizing Your Plot: On the Backbone of Fiction

*By Jeff Chapman*

Have you ever ridden a roller coaster? Have you ever watched anyone riding a roller coaster? Thrill seekers line up, anticipating a heart-stopping plunge with enough g-force to temporarily rearrange their inner organs. Before the final loop or dive, riders anticipate a series of smaller climbs and falls leading up to the big one. If the ride meets or exceeds expectations, riders will stumble from the cars, praising the experience to their friends as they ask for help to get back in line for another go.

A story has much in common with a roller coaster, and a reader has much in common with a thrill seeker, except readers don't want their stomachs lodged between their ears. When someone begins reading a story, they expect a series of increasingly difficult complications leading to a climax and resolution. The writer has a contract with readers, as a roller coaster operator has a contract with riders.

Ignore or violate that contract at your peril. Imagine an amusement park ride with the most thrilling dive at the beginning followed by a slow deceleration to a gentle stop. How many riders would jump out before the end? Imagine a story with the most exciting, tension-filled events in the first scene. How many readers would close the book before the end? How many would feel cheated after the last line?

**Story Structure Basics**

For the past couple of years, I've been studying story structure. Witty dialogue, sympathetic characters and shiny sentences won't do the writer much good without a compelling story to inhabit. Writers don't consistently turn out great stories by accident. The secret, which isn't much of a secret, is story structure.

The plots of stories that *work*, that is, pull the reader through the story and satisfy the reader's expectations, follow a similar structure, regardless of genre. There are many ways to divide, name, and define the parts of a story. You may find some people are passionate about a particular method. I suggest you read widely on story structure, borrow from various experts, and use what makes the most sense to you.

I prefer to think of stories as having three parts.

First comes the inciting incident and point of no return. Some event interrupts normal life and the protagonist decides to commit to a course of action to remedy a problem.

Second comes the middle build, a rising series of complications and conflicts in which the protagonist wrestles with the problem.

Third comes the climax and resolution in which you pay off the expectations raised in the first act.

Let's see how the three-part structure works with some examples. Consider Agatha Christie's *Murder on the Orient Express*. The inciting incident is the late-night murder of Samuel Ratchett, who occupies the compartment next to Hercule Poirot. In addition to the turmoil caused by the murder, snow on the track has stranded the train. M. Bouc, the director of the train line and a friend to Poirot, asks Poirot to investigate while they wait for the track to be cleared. Poirot accepts, committing himself to solve the problem of the murder. During the second part, Poirot searches for clues in the victim's compartment, interviews the passengers, and considers events he witnessed on the train before the murder. The passengers suggest that Ratchett, who has been shown to be the notorious child-murderer Lanfranco Cassetti, was the target of a mafia hit. The assailant, they argue, secretly boarded and left the train. Some physical evidence seems to support this interpretation but other evidence casts doubt. In the third part, Poirot gathers the passengers and proposes two theories: an assassination by an unknown assailant or an execution carried out by all the passengers as revenge for Cassetti's crimes. Poirot reviews the evidence for the assembled passengers and concludes that only the second theory fits the evidence. Christie has explained the crime and paid off reader's expectations.

Consider a fantasy adventure story such as *The Hobbit* by J.R.R. Tolkien. The arrival of Gandalf and the dwarves serves as the inciting incident. When Bilbo finally accepts their offer and joins the expedition to the Lonely Mountain, we enter the middle build. Bilbo and friends suffer numerous mishaps and near escapes. After the death of Smaug, a dragon, the dwarves take control of the mountain and its hidden treasure. But Smaug's death is not the climax. It is the doorway to part three. During the middle build, the dwarves have dealings with goblins, Wood-elves, and the men of Lake-town, leaving "unpaid debts" in their wake. The climax comes with The Battle of Five Armies, in which the goblins suffer defeat and the dwarves heal their relations with the Lake-men and Wood-elves. Bilbo returns home, richer in body, mind, and spirit. From the inciting incident, the reader expects a dangerous journey and a fight with a dragon. Those expectations have been paid off with interest.

**Plotting Your Plot**

I find visualizing a concept helps me to understand it and see multiple relationships at once. You can see the climbs, crests and falls of a roller coaster. With some graph paper and a pencil, you can do the same with your plot. Along the vertical axis, make a scale of one to 10. These numbers correspond to the level of tension in a scene relative to the other scenes in the story. Along the horizontal axis, list the scenes in the story. Determine the lowest and highest level of tension in each scene relative to the other scenes in the story and mark these points on the graph. A well-developed scene will mimic the three-part structure of the overall story, so many scenes may have a wide range in their tension level. Alternatively, you could plot three points for each scene: the tension level for the beginning, climax, and resolution. When all the scenes have been plotted, connect the dots.

You should see a graph that resembles a roller coaster with rises and falls. The overall pattern should steadily rise toward the high-point, the story's climax, and then descend with the resolution. What you don't want to see are long stretches of low tension. Will readers become bored? Are these stretches in which nothing important is happening? The purpose of this exercise is to step back from your story's details and think about its flow from a high level. The graph is a diagnostic tool.

Let's consider a real-world example. *Carmilla,* published by J. Sheridan Le Fanu in 1871-72, is my favorite vampire tale. Like many horror stories, the protagonist gradually accumulates knowledge of a threat until the danger is unmasked and dispatched in the nick of time. This first-person novella comprises sixteen chapters, which I'll treat as the scenes to plot. I give higher scores to incidents in which the protagonist suffers physical and emotional trauma. Below is a list of the chapters and their scores along with my reasoning behind the score. These are not by any means full summaries of each chapter. The scores are impressionistic. We could quibble over them, but I believe the pattern of rising and falling tension building to a climax will remain.

Chapter 1: Score 7

Laura recalls an incident from her childhood in which a strange woman attacked her in her sleep.

Chapter 2: Score 1

Laura and her father witness a carriage accident which leads to a young woman named Carmilla being placed with them. Laura is happy to have a new potential friend.

Chapter 3: Score 6

Laura suffers a shock when she visits Carmilla's room and finds she looks exactly like the strange woman who attacked her as a child.

Chapter 4: Score 3

Laura describes Carmilla's habits and physical languor. We also learn that a strange illness is sweeping the neighborhood and several peasants have died.

Chapter 5: Score 2

A portrait, over a century old, is returned to Laura's father after cleaning. The portrait of Countess Mircalla looks exactly like Carmilla. Laura thinks the likeness is a small miracle and is pleased to have the portrait.

Chapter 6: Score 8

Laura is attacked in the night by some creature that bites her chest.

Chapter 7: Score 9

Laura grows progressively weaker. One night she wakes to see Carmilla at the foot of her bed drenched in blood.

Chapter 8: Score 7

Laura discovers that Carmilla is not in her room although the door is locked. The house and grounds are searched to no avail. Later in the day, Carmilla turns up in her room with no explanation for her disappearance.

Chapter 9: Score 6

Laura's father calls in a doctor to examine Laura. The doctor examines the puncture wounds and suggests steps to take. Laura is concerned about being ill.

Chapter 10: Score 2

On way to a picnic in the ruins of an old castle, Laura and father meet General Spielsdorf on his way to visit them.

Chapter 11: Score 4

General Spielsdorf tells the story of a ball and how his ward made a new friend.

Chapter 12: Score 5

General Spielsdorf tells how his ward's new friend came to stay with them.

Chapter 13: Score 6

General Spielsdorf describes the symptoms of his ward's fatal illness and claims that Countess Mircalla (from the portrait) is a vampire. The General's story sounds eerily similar to Laura's experiences with Carmilla. Laura recognizes that her symptoms are the same as those of the General's ward.

Chapter 14: Score 10

General Spielsdorf describes Mircalla's last attack on his ward and the young girl's death. Carmilla arrives at the ruins for the picnic. The General declares that Carmilla is the vampire Mircalla. The two fight and Carmilla escapes.

Chapter 15: Score 4

The hidden grave of Mircalla is found, the body exumed, and the vampire dispatched.

Chapter 16: Score 2

Laura reflects on the nature of vampires and how her encounter with Carmilla has tainted the rest of her life.

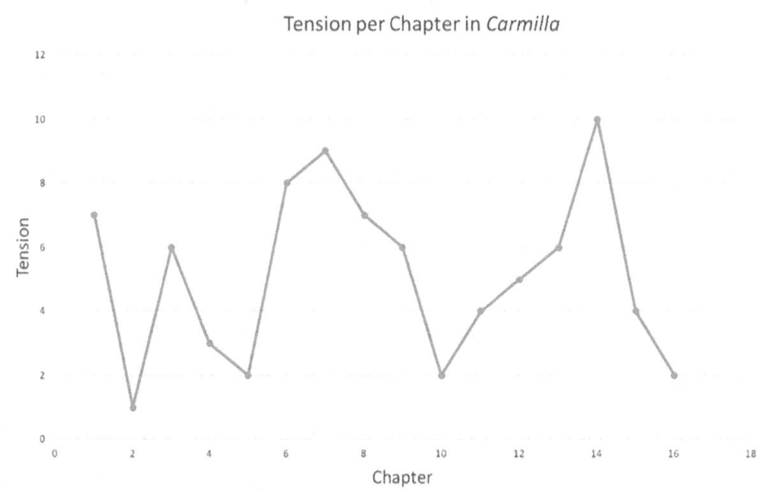


**Figure 1.** *Tension per Chapter in* Carmilla.

**Recommended Resources on Story Structure**

Understanding story structure is critical to your success as a writer. Here are a few book recommendations to begin your studies.

*The Story Grid: What Good Editors Know* by Shawn Coyne (Black Irish Entertainment LLC, 2015). In this book Coyne details his system for analyzing story structure. Coyne has years of experience as an editor for New York publishing houses. Although most of his examples focus on thrillers, the concepts and lessons are universal.

*Write Great Fiction—Plot & Structure* (Writer's Digest Books, 5th ed., 2004) and *Elements of Fiction Writing: Conflict and Suspense* by James Scott Bell (Writer's Digest Books, 2012). Bell is a well-known suspense writer who has also written many books on story craft. His explanations in these two books are very accessible. He also provides numerous examples as well as tips for fixing problems.

*The Art of Fiction: Notes on Craft for Young Writers* by John Gardner (Vintage, reissue edition, 2001). A novelist, medievalist and well-known teacher of writing, Gardner pulls examples from literary works in his examination of story structure.

*Take Off Your Pants!: Outline Your Books for Faster, Better Writing* by Libbie Hawker (Running Rabbit Press, 2nd edition, 2015). A writer of historical and literary fiction, Hawker focuses on character arcs and describes using the hero's journey as a structuring guide.

I hope you find visualizing your plot and the book recommendations beneficial to your development. Go forth and write some great stories.

# The Magic of Good Characterization

*By Susie Finkbeiner*

It's never a good idea to chuck a hardbound book across the room. They're heavy enough to dent the wall, scuff the paint and severely disturb the cat. In all circumstances, it is ill-advised to disturb the cat.

Fortunately, it's been more than a few years since I've flung a book (much to the relief of the calico). I do, however, remember the exact book I lobbed.

It was one I'd long anticipated, one with a premise that should have wowed me at every turn of the page. The narrative was well written. There was plenty of action and a plot line that didn't slow down. I should have liked the book. Alas, I did not.

It took me until the second half of the story to realize why I wasn't enjoying the read. In the story it was revealed that there was a bomb. The whole gaggle of characters were at risk of being blown to smithereens. And I didn't care in the least if they did.

That was when I realized that I'd been reading a fantastic plot peopled with a cast of cardboard cut-out characters.

Whiz, bang, plop, hiss. The book flew across the room, banged on the wall, and fell to the floor. The cat was disturbed.

**Flesh, Bone, and Maybe a Little Junk-In-The-Trunk**

There is nothing that can keep a reader from engaging in a story as much as a poorly developed cast of characters. Conversely, characters who breathe and move and have a little roundness to them will pull a reader right into the fiction.

As writers, it is our job to put flesh on the bones of our characters. We must give them shape, bulk and weight so that our readers suspend their disbelief. The goal is for the characters to be so real that the reader feels something for them (whether that be love or hate). It is the gift we give to readers. The magic of good characterization.

Have you ever cried for a character? Prayed for him or her? Found yourself thinking of a character and wondering how she or he is?

That, my friend, is the sign of a well-written character.

**The Must-Haves of Good Characters**

While there is no formula for writing well rounded characters, there are elements essential to making them fully realized. We find these nuts and bolts of characterization in literature across genres and throughout the history of the written word.

1. **Physical Description:** This seems like the most basic of characterization tools, but it is also a fantastic way to show rather than tell. But don't just throw in generic details, try to insert *telling details*. Even the smallest physical cue can provide insight into your character's personality, struggles, or aspirations.

John Irving's Owen Meany is abnormally small and of harsh voice, both of which prove essential to the novel's plot. Anne Shirley of Green Gables fame is known for her red hair which sets her apart for teasing, but also helps her grow in strength of personality. Harry Potter's lightning-shaped scar tells the story of his past of which he has no memory.

A character's looks can demonstrate so much about him or her and add dimension. A note, however: physical descriptions are often overdone. Only let us see what is essential for us to know.

2. **Emotional Makeup:** More important than how they look is how characters respond emotionally to diverse circumstances. If annoyed, do they blow a gasket? Do they clam up when confronted? How do they respond to the death of a loved one? What does their emotional response indicate about the kind of person they are? The history they lived? Do they default to fight or flight? Why might that be?

Dorian Gray pouts and throws a fit when he is denied something he wants. Doug Swieteck from *Okay for Now* buries his emotions as a defense mechanism. Annie Wilkes from *Misery* swings from one extreme to the other with little to no provocation.

How does the writer determine the emotional constitution of a character? By asking "what if" and writing what seems most true. That is when the writer will discover an element which not only establishes a character, but also drives the plot forward.

3. **History:** Let's say you meet someone at a writers' conference. The moment you shake hands is not the very moment that person is born into

existence. That person enjoys a history, unique experiences and years of day-to-day occurrences which inform who he or she is. The same is true for your characters.

Every character has a backstory. And those unique backstories comprise the reasons for how they speak, react, relate and decide.

Jay Gatsby's every move in *The Great Gatsby* is an effort to put in the past his humble beginnings, as well as attain the love of Daisy. Johnny Nolan from *A Tree Grows in Brooklyn* comes from a long line of alcoholics who die early, and while he desires to overcome that history, he is unable to. August Pullman from *Wonder* is not only different because of how he was born, but is a loving and empathetic person because of how his parents raised him.

Consider how where you grew up influenced how you speak, how your name reflects your personality, or the way events in your childhood formed you into the adult you are today. It's the same for your characters. History is what makes a written person take on depth of personality.

As with physical description, use backstory with a light hand in your narrative. While it's essential for the author to know the full history, it may not be beneficial to the reader to be so overwhelmed.

4. **Strengths and Vulnerabilities**: Superman can fly, see through brick walls and can freeze things with a puff of breath. He has super strength and skills, but then there's always kryptonite which can render him into a puddle on the floor. It's uninteresting to read about a character who is strong without a hint of weakness. However, when we see a character's vulnerabilities, we can relate. They feel more authentic—substantial and real.

Scout Finch from *To Kill a Mockingbird* is a determined, brave and loyal girl who is also headstrong to a fault. While her personality is strong, her vulnerability is her youth and ignorance to how the adult world works (especially when adults behave badly). The mythic figure Achilles is immortal and unbeatable—that is, unless he's struck on his heel. Elizabeth Bennet from *Pride and Prejudice* is level headed and intelligent, however her dysfunctional life at home proves to be her vulnerability.

Think of every real-life person you know. They each house within them strengths and weaknesses, as do you. Writing such complexity into your characters will make them relatable and authentic.

4. **Relationships:** The great poet John Donne said that "no man is an island entire of itself; every man is a piece of the continent, part of the

main..."[12] He was right. We all interact and relate to others in our lives. Even a hermit has known at least one person. We are formed by our relationships with family, friends, enemies, and such. So it should be with our characters.

Frodo Baggins has Samwise. Harry Potter has Ron and Hermione. Holden Caulfield has all the phonies at his school in *The Catcher in the Rye*. The Joads have an old jalopy full of family, a preacher and a shifty son-in-law in *The Grapes of Wrath*. Hester Prynne doesn't just have a scarlet letter, she has her daughter Pearl. Scout Finch has Boo Radley.

Our characters' relationships sharpen them and help them to grow. They can also serve to oppose them and challenge them. Sometimes they even lead our characters astray. Like in our lives, friends, family, and enemies help make us who we are.

5. **Motivation:** Kurt Vonnegut once said, "Every character should want something, even if it's only a glass of water."[13] What is it that your characters want more than anything else? This is the question you must ask before you even write one word of the story. Additionally, you must ask it in regards to each character you write. After you find that out, you will discover what your characters will do in order to get what they want.

We see this element in all the great and unforgettable characters in fiction. Katniss Everdeen from *The Hunger Games* is willing to volunteer for a savage "game" in order to protect her sister. Shakespeare's Macbeth wants to be king so badly he's willing to betray and kill. Curley from *Of Mice and Men* so desires to be seen as strong he's willing to be cruel.

Learning what a character wants will not only add depth to the persons of the story, it will also drive the plot, which makes your job a whole lot easier.

6. **Conflict (both external and internal):** We all know that a story about a man wanting a glass of water and getting it with no struggle would be dull. There must be conflict—both external and internal—which prevents the character from getting right away what he or she wants. The man wants a glass of water but knows there's a shortage. He must travel a day's journey through a dangerous land to get it (this is external conflict). But he knows that any water he finds would belong to a family who needs it, too. He'd be writing the death sentence of that family in order to get that glass of water (this is internal conflict).

---

12 Donne, John. "No Man is an Island." *Devotions upon Emergent Occasions*, 1624

13 Vonnegut, Kurt. *Bagombo Snuff Box: Uncollected Short Fiction*. Berkley, August 2000.

Babe from Dick King-Smith's classic children's book wants to be a sheepherder, but he's a pig. Katniss Everdeen wants to return to her family, but has 23 other teens to fight to the death before she can (and she doesn't want to kill). A character untested is a character undeveloped. They must have hurdles to jump, dragons to slay, and demons to outrun in order to have any kind of substance.

7. **Moral Compass:** One thing we need to know about our characters—both protagonists and antagonists—is what morals direct their course. What do they value? What code to they stick to? Do they hold to a list of rules or are they trying to break as many as they can?

Atticus Finch (yes, you may all swoon if you must) is driven by what is just and fair. Voldemort (okay, shudder if you must) will do anything within his power to have supremacy. Not every character is as extreme as these two examples, but we'll get into more complexity in a moment. The point here is that a character's moral compass provides rich internal conflict for your protagonist which will deepen your story.

8. **Complexity:** When writers craft a character who is either all good or all bad, they have failed to provide roundness and depth. This is a shame of the highest literary degree. As humans, we have this duality within each of us. So should our fictional beings.

I can think of few other characters quite as complex as Severus Snape from the Harry Potter series. He absolutely hates Harry, yet he protects him. His past is one of darkness and yet he has turned from that old life. He is at once villain and hero, darkness and light, champion and adversary. Readers of these books hate him and love him all at the same time. And by the last book of the series, they are reduced to tears because his character is so very real.

When a character embodies both good and bad, battling between the two throughout the story, there is nothing which will engage a reader more.

### To Write Better Characters You Must Read Better Characters

Now that you know some of the tools of characterization, it's time to crack open a book (or, even better, a whole bunch of books). I've found that the very best way to learn about writing round, full, flesh-and-blood characters is to read. Widely, wildly, eclectically and critically.

Read across genres and put aside your preferences to try something you otherwise might not. Ask for book recommendations from friends who are well-read. Discover a new author at your local bookstore. Ask your librarians what their favorite novels are. And read, friends. Read.

There is no better writers' workshop than the open book. Keep a notebook with you to jot down ideas of what works in these characters you read, even to make note of what doesn't. Writers read. It's how we learn and grow and hold onto our sense of wonder.

**Back to the Flying Book, the Disturbed Cat, and Putting on Shoes**

While I regret throwing the book and, in so doing, uprooting the cat from her comfortable sunspot, I do not hate that I read that book. Spending time with characters who did not ring true taught me to be more aware of the fictional people with whom I populate my stories. It inspired within me the determination to craft authentic characters, not caricatures. I learned how valuable it is to spend the time refining, developing and fully realizing my protagonist, antagonist, and even secondary and incidental characters.

And when we do give life to these real, breathing, authentic characters we are doing a great service to our readers. We are setting a pair of shoes before them, inviting them to slip their feet in. We offer readers the chance to see the world in a new and awe inspiring way. As they step into those shoes we give them the gift of knowing that they are not alone.

This is the magic of good characterization.

# Injecting Real Life into Fiction—Even if Your Life is Decidedly Normal

*By Zachary Bartels*

The world is constantly trying to divide us into two groups: Type A personality or Type B, hoarders or purgers, liberals or conservatives. Most of these are false dichotomies, in my experience, as real people land somewhere on a continuum between the two extremes (or maybe even off the continuum altogether). The same thing is true of the dichotomies applied to writers. One example: plotters vs. pantsers (someone who develops a plot while "flying by the seat of their pants"). I assembled a 12,000-word "outline" involving three poster boards and seven different color codes for my second novel, but most of these details were first written in my head (pantser-style) and excitedly spewed into a digital voice recorder before being transcribed. So, which am I?

I've always known I was neither a slave to an outline nor a free-associating, structure-less traceur of the pen. But I admit that, until recently, I did believe in a different literary dichotomy: those who write what they know versus those who write what they want to read. These two clichés seemed mutually exclusive to me, and I've always assumed that I fall decidedly into the second category.

Let me explain. My books are probably best classified as "supernatural thrillers." When I was doing publicity for my first novel, *Playing Saint,* I did about fifty radio interviews. And in almost every case, the interviewer skimmed my bio (pastor, Bible teacher) and the copy for the book (demon possession, serial killers, cops, Vatican agents), and asked, "How does a guy like you wind up writing something like *this?*" And every time, I answered, drily, "Oh, this is just an account of my average Wednesday." Yes, I was so far away from "write what you know" that it became a punchline I returned to again and again. Despite being a man of the cloth, my life is anything but a supernatural thriller.

But then I had an epiphany about a year ago: this dichotomy is false as well. We *all* write what we know to some degree. We can't help it. And the more we own it and hone it—the more we intentionally leverage it—the better our writing would be. This set me on a months-long journey of reading books and articles, assessing my own writing process and experimenting with different approaches. Here's what I discovered.

**Inject What You Know Into What You Write**

If you're John Grisham, this is obvious. You know the legal system and you draw on that knowledge and experience several times per page, resulting in yet another *New York Times* bestseller. But even if you're writing way outside your field, you can inject what you know into what you write. And if done right, the effect is a book, essay, or short story that feels a lot more "real."

I used to be obsessed with this yogurt called "Simplait," whose gimmick was that it only contained five ingredients, one of them being natural fruit flavoring. I always got the strawberry and it tasted so rich, so real, that when they stopped making it, I worried what the withdrawal would do to my psyche. I knew I couldn't go back to those other yogurts with the fake strawberry flavor, which doesn't even taste like actual strawberry. Did you know the primary ingredient in artificial berry flavor comes from a beaver's anal gland? I'm not joking—look it up. And what about the fake banana flavor used in candy? It's not even close to the taste of a real banana! More like hot plastic.

Likewise, we're all familiar with the tropes used in police procedurals (whether on-screen or on the pulp page), and we can identify them immediately, but only in the way we can identify grape soda—because we've encountered it before, not because it tastes even remotely like a real grape. In order to avoid that "artificial flavors" taste in your writing, you've got to inject something real—something natural—into your characters, plot and setting. And where do you get this natural flavor? From what you *know*. And I don't just mean what you know *about*. I mean what you know in the relational sense—the way you know your good friends.

This might be a slam-dunk for you. Perhaps your life experience (whether in the Marine Corps, the Peace Corps or battling cancer) naturally translates to the written page. My friend Carrie Stuart Parks has created a successful series, drawing largely on her own experience as a forensic artist for the FBI. My friend Cliff Graham has drawn on his extensive military experience to flesh out bestselling novels about biblical warriors and the battles they fought. Me, I worked in a cubicle and attended seminary for a decade. Since then I've done a lot of funerals, drank a lot of Red Bull and smoked a lot of cigars. And I can recite entire episodes of the '80s comedy *Family Ties*. So, yeah, on the surface, my life does not exactly lend itself to engaging storytelling. So how do I inject what I know into what I want to read? Perhaps a couple of examples.

I admit that, while I pretended to be humoring my wife every Sunday night for five years, I was actually a pretty big fan of *Downton Abbey*. Why? Because it really felt like I was transported to another world—one about which I knew very little. How did Julian Fellowes, who lives in the same modern world that you and I do, so perfectly capture the bygone dynamic of post-Edwardian aristocratic living, as experienced by servants, lords and everyone in between? Because he *knows* the stuff. And not just knows *about it*. He's clearly immersed himself in the topic so much that it's become real to him and that *realness* bleeds over onto the page and, from there, onto the screen.

My dad is the same way with the Civil War. Growing up, many of our family trips involved taking a longer route that would bring us by a Civil War battlefield. Dad would get out of the car and look at this open space and know what had happened there. The way he talked about it revealed that he did not see the Walmart in the distance or the empty Combos bag floating in the breeze. He saw Chamberlain and his men (or whoever) preparing to charge or defend their position.

As for me, I know the Bible, and that factors heavily into what I've written. I know snarky humor and pop culture references, which also make their way into my work. And I know the life of a pastor. My first novel began as a straightforward cop story that I was trying to write. But it wouldn't pop. Off-and-on I wrote at this thing for years, but it always seemed too obvious, too derivative and too detached. It was only when I added a pastor character as a fish-out-of-water through which the reader experiences the story that the book came together. My life is nothing like Parker Saint's, but he gave me a point of connection with everything else in the story. "As a pastor, what would be my instinct here? How would I react?" It allowed me to color what I wanted to read with what I knew.

And that's what Grisham does as well, isn't it? I guarantee that guy has never narrowly avoided a car bomb, just as Fellowes has never had to surreptitiously move a Turkish diplomat's body through a large estate to protect the honor of a pseudo-heiress. But there's enough natural flavoring drawn from the writers' lives and injected into both stories to sell them convincingly.

And this can be done tangentially too. My former secretary spent years as a legal secretary at a big downtown law firm during the *Mad Men* era. And believe me, she had stories. If she were so inclined, she could write a great book about her experiences, altered only to protect herself from lawsuits. Or she could write a sort of tell-all story about a lawyer in that era, changing up the cases and places, but keeping the candid authenticity, because she knows what makes them tick—how they think, talk and act—even better than they do.

**Dig Deeper**

And that leads me to the idea of injecting my *internal life* into what I write. My life is not just a set of experiences; it's also my response to those experiences. You may not think your life is worthy of literary attention, but you *do have* all sorts of things going on inside of you that *are* very interesting. They're just waiting to be discovered. Human emotion and instinct and struggle are universal, and can be transferred into your story fairly easily.

I was doing this without even realizing it, and you probably are too. For example, that sarcastic answer I gave to the repeated interview question evolved over time. Eventually, I would answer by saying, "It's just an average Wednesday," (pause for chuckle) and then add, "But there really is something autobiographical about the book. Because, as a minister, I feel this constant struggle between wanting to be a faithful shepherd and wanting to be successful by the world's metrics." And that struggle very much fed into the story. I asked myself, "What would that internal tension look like if I externalized it and made it a conflict in someone's life?"

We are full of these tensions and inner-struggles, but few people are really in touch with them anymore. Drawing on such things is a lost art. Today, when we feel some angst inside, most people just pull out their smartphone (aka pacifier for grownups) and Maggie Simpson that thing by playing some Kwazy Cupcakes or scrolling through their Facebook feed until the feelings die back down. But you have the option of leaving the iPhone in your pocket and *feeling* that discomfort for a minute, experiencing it, and *writing it down*. Because what you've got there is gold! It's the kind of ingredient that can make a story *great*.

If you are able to leverage this well enough, you can write compellingly about even the mundane every-day, as-is. Writer Harvey Pekar did this for years in his cult-classic comic *American Splendor.* People clamored for his observational insights, couched in stories from the not-so-fascinating-or-fast-paced world of working in a medical records office.

But again, you can apply this straight-on or laterally. The question becomes, how can I take that tension I'm feeling and apply it to a lawyer or a politician or a stay-at-home parent (who wants to be liked by his or her child but also wants to be faithful to the task of raising up a responsible child)? Rather than guess what my characters might feel, I can inject a little of my own tension into them and let them feel it after me.

I think one of the best examples of this is Chuck Palahnuik. I once heard an interview in which he told of his experience of grief after his father was murdered. He had this urge as he drove home one night after identifying his father's body to stop his car on the shoulder of the road, leave the headlights on and just lie there in the beams of light until someone wearing a uniform came along to help him and told him everything would be okay. He spun this off in a tangent, resulting in the book *Choke,* about a guy who forces himself to choke on food at restaurants so that a stranger would give him the Heimlich, which is pictured as this sort of life-giving hug—the only way the character could experience real, meaningful human contact and compassion.

**Jot It Down!**

Much of what you can inject into your writing is emotional or sensory flash paper. If you don't write it down in the moment, it may slip through your fingers forever. That's why I carry at least one digital recorder (in addition to my phone) everywhere I go and even have a pad of water-proof paper in my shower.

I jot down every little detail that might stand in as a part for a whole. (e.g. "Every surface in the DMV is sticky.") I find these details incredibly helpful for filling out settings and characters. I think of it as injecting aspects of places and people I know into what I write. I've even been known to pair up a character with a real-life friend or acquaintance. I promise, they'll never be the wiser.

My second book was called *The Last Con* and one of my favorite characters was a mob enforcer named Marcus Brinkman. Now, I don't know any mob enforcers. But I know a guy who *could be* a mob enforcer. And, while I was writing, I observed every little thing I could about this guy: how he stood, how he dressed, his verbal tics.

When I first started a Facebook "author page" years ago, one of my old college professors commented, "This is exciting for you. Just be sure you don't use your parishioners' lives for inspiration." And I was like, "No. I'll just be sure I don't get *caught*." Because we have to draw on real people unless we want our writing to have that hot-plastic taste of artificial banana, rather than the refreshing flavor of the real thing. Usually this amounts to *mining*, not full-formed characters, but individual traits. It's like dressing a set with "props" from your own living room.

After *Playing Saint* came out, a few friends of mine said, "I think I know who you were basing this particular character on," and named a well-known religious figure from Grand Rapids. And maybe they were right. I'm not saying I did and I'm not saying I didn't. What I am saying is that the little disclaimer your publisher puts on the copyright page—the one that says "any similarity to any real persons living or dead is purely coincidental"—is a lie. *Any similarity* is coincidental? No it's not! Almost every little quirk, trait, and idiom is drawn from *someone* we've encountered. And that person is, by process of elimination, either living or dead.

And hopefully, if we're coloring what we want to read with what we know and what we've experienced, our writing will strike the reader as a lot more living than dead.

# A Picture is Worth a Thousand Words: What Fiction Writers Can Learn From Screenwriters

*By Thomas McClurg*

I love movies, and yet for all the enjoyment I gain from immersing myself in an expertly crafted film, it is the act of writing fiction that calls to me. No matter what part of the storytelling journey you're on, tight storytelling is a difficult beast to wrangle into submission. Consider screenwriters. They've got actors and special effects and makeup departments and lighting specialists all helping to bring their scripts to life. Yet even with all these resources at their disposal, numerous films receive bad reviews or fail at the box office. But a well-made film is an experience worth savoring again and again.

It's that experience we storytellers hope to create.

It's been said "a picture is worth a thousand words." Screenwriters need every one of them to pull their weight. Movies take us from humble beginnings to epic victory in an hour and a half. As prose writers, we have more freedom. We can tell a story over hundreds of pages. But with that freedom comes the danger of churning out heaps of words in an effort to paint the pictures that movies provide so easily.

In our zeal to dazzle our reader's imagination with scintillating verbal brush strokes, we risk the opposite effect. Words pile up like sand in an hourglass and the story gets buried—a treasure hidden beneath all those words. We want to be clear story tellers. We want to unearth that buried treasure and help our readers get lost in the worlds we create.

This isn't a chapter on screenwriting, but rather, some of the ways I have found the discipline of screenwriting to be beneficial to my growth as a fiction writer.

**Discipline in Description**

There's something about writing a story that fills you with a sense of ultimate power. You are the master of the universe. You create and destroy with impunity, and your characters dance at your every whim, but sometimes that power can lead to undisciplined writing. We churn out pages and pages of description as we breathe life into scenes and characters, and since everything we write comes from the purest well springs of our creative souls, trimming that description down can sometimes feel like being forced to amputate a limb. But amputate we must.

This is an area screenplays can provide a wonderful example.

Screenplays are a more confining medium than novels. While a novel can have hundreds of pages, a screenplay should be between 90-120 pages long, depending on the genre. The rule of thumb is that one page of script translates to one minute of screen time. So comedies are in the 90-page range, while big budget action flicks are closer to 120 pages long. And this is not 90-to-120 pages of dense text. Scripts are strictly formatted to include lots of white space between scene headings, action, dialogue and description. And yet, a screenwriter is still expected to write evocative scene descriptions. In fact, I have heard it said that many screenwriters are encouraged to use no more than four lines when describing a scene.

The screenplay for the movie *Alien* is an extreme example. The first shot, a look inside the engine room of a starship is described with exactly two words: "Empty, cavernous."

Then the writer moves on.

Check out the screenplay sometime. You can find it online. The *Alien* script is unusually spartan, even for screenwriting, but it's viewed as something screenwriters should work toward: writing clear description using the fewest words possible, the right words.

As a fun exercise, try writing chunks of description for different people or places from one of your stories. Try to make it as clear and colorful as you can without going over four lines. Not four sentences, four *lines*. Then try whittling that back to three, then two, then one. Just for fun. See what happens, enjoy the challenge and give your creative mind a workout.

**Trim Down Your Scenes**

There's a saying in screen writing that "movies move." Action is the focus whether that action is physical or emotional or psychological. If the screenplay drags at any moment, it's the kiss of death. Each scene is like a fire cracker. You light the fuse and run for cover. There's a delay and then...*bang!*

Imagine a scene in which a SWAT team is called to bust some criminals:

The call is made and the team assembles. They load up and drive to the location. Maybe you see the team members in the back of the truck checking their weapons or getting briefed on how the operation will go down.

They arrive, work their way up the stairs to the right room, get into position, and bust in. Chaos ensues and the bad guys are apprehended. They take the bad guys downstairs, throw them into the back of a police car and haul them away to the station.

End scene.

The fuse is lit the moment they get the call. That's where the scene starts, but it doesn't really explode until they bust through the door and take down the baddies. After that it's all clean up.

The goal is to start the scene as close to the bang as possible and then move to the next scene without delay. Light too long of a fuse and the audience might get bored before the bang. Take too long to clean up and the audience might get bored before the next bang arrives. Just like a good movie keeps things moving forward at a swift pace, we want to grab our reader's attention and keep it for the duration of the story.

So let's imagine the scene again, but let's cut the fuse a bit. Start the scene with the SWAT team right outside the door, or better yet, start the scene with them kicking down the door.

Bang! The audience is thrust into the action.

Then instead of watching the SWAT team haul the bad guys away, imagine we cut the scene right after they slap on the cuffs or even right after they pin them to the ground. The scene accomplishes what it needs to do. We see the bad guys apprehended. We get into the action swiftly and leave with the smell of gunpowder fresh in our noses, eager for more. In and out. Quick and effective.

The same mentality can be applied to fiction and can go a long way to keeping the reader turning pages. This doesn't mean that every scene is nothing but an explosion; it means we are jumping into what's important faster, showing the important action, and leaving the scene so we can move to the next important part of the story without letting the action lag.

Take a look at your scenes. Are there fuses that could be cut? Once you've set a scene in motion, does it take a long time to get to the next bang?

**Focus On What Matters Most**

Imagine you're watching a movie. The camera goes into a home. It pans around the rooms, makes its way to the living room and focuses on a picture hanging on the wall. It's a man in a military uniform. The picture looks old. The uniform is dated. The camera moves to the right. Another picture. Another man in uniform. Newer than the first, but still old. The camera keeps moving to the right. More pictures of men in military uniforms. The pictures gradually become newer and more modern. At the end of the row of pictures is a nail in the wall right where a new picture would fit but the spot is empty. After looking at the pictures, the camera moves to a small open display case with a red velvet lining. There are several medals resting in the case alongside a gun. It's a revolver with a decorative handle. There's an engraving on the handle. The camera holds position on the gun. Holding, holding, and holding until it finally moves outside and to the house next door where we meet the real focus of the story. The first house and the pictures and the gun are never seen again.

At best you feel confused, at worst you feel betrayed, right? The simple fact that the camera focused on the pictures and the gun made you believe they were important. If that scene had made it into a movie, and all those items failed to be important we would feel cheated, defrauded by the writer and director. There's a good chance we would lose trust in their ability to handle the material, and, as a result, we disengage from the story.

That scene would be quickly cut from any final draft. It just wasn't necessary or related to the story being told. Proper formatting for any well-constructed script involves ranking the important details. The screenwriter lets the director know what to focus on, and the director carries that vision to the audience.

Take characters for example. If they are in the background and don't have speaking roles they are extras. They don't get names, or any focus whatsoever.

If they have lines and play a minor role in a given scene they are required to be played by paid actors. They are then given names like ANGRY MECHANIC or NERVOUS THUG.

If they have more than a few lines and play a larger role they become minor characters and would likely be given actual names like STEVE or JESSICA.

Minor characters move up to supporting characters and then main characters. Each group should be well-designed and well-rendered, but the amount of time used to describe what they say and how they say it, or how they are dressed, or any of the other details that go with them is regulated by the role they play in the story. Screenwriters cannot afford to waste words describing a minor character when they are needed to describe a main character, no matter how interesting the minor character might be to the writer.

The same is true when writing fiction. Consider the following scene:

Max wove his way through the crowded marketplace, sliding sideways like a snake slithering through cracks in the human blockade. A merchant held up a freshly caught fish so large it took two hands to hoist it aloft. His sleeves were rolled up to the elbow exposing sunbaked forearms pockmarked with small scars, no doubt the result of years of handling fishhooks. His wide face had a fresh layer of stubble and his long black hair was pulled back and tied in a tail. His whole body swayed as he displayed the fish for all to see. It was an almost graceful motion coming from a man who was likely accustomed to moving about with the world shifting beneath his feet. The merchant looked at Max and yelled, "Just pulled this beauty out of the water! Come take a closer look!" Max gave him a sidelong glance and moved on.

If this scene was part of a full length novel, this would be the only time the reader sees the fish merchant, but with so much effort being used to describe him, anyone reading this in a story would naturally assume he is important. With each digested detail, the reader forms a picture and attaches greater and greater significance to the merchant. Surely any character worth so many words must play an important role at some point in the story? The reader will eagerly await the merchant's involvement in the story. When he fails to be important, it will diminish your credibility as an author in the mind of the reader. The next time something is actually important, the reader will be hesitant to make that connection because of the times where you did not deliver on an unspoken contract, a contract that states what you focus on is actually important to the story and therefore worth their time and attention.

The scene would be better served as something like this:

Max wove his way through the crowded marketplace, sliding sideways like a snake slithering through cracks in the human blockade. A merchant held up a freshly caught fish and yelled, "Just pulled this beauty out of the water! Come take a closer look!" Max gave him a sidelong glance and moved on.

The merchant adds a bit of color to the setting, but that's it. No description needed and the reader's focus remains squarely where it belongs, on Max.

This can be challenging. When I'm writing I can be easily distracted by a place or person or object in my head. I want to describe every detail because writing is fun and my imagination eagerly carries me away. But writing like this is undisciplined and obscures the story. It might seem counter intuitive to cut out details to tell a clearer story, but removing the words that don't belong will thrust the ones that do belong directly into the spotlight, allowing them to shine all the brighter.

**Fade Out**

Part of the fun of being a writer is the continuous learning process we all undertake; the search for that little nugget that will turn on a light bulb and force us to look at a project in new and exciting ways.

Along my own writing journey, I have picked up numerous such nuggets from the exploration of screenwriting, and I treasure each and every one of them. Some books I recommend are: *Your Screenplay Sucks!: 100 Ways to Make it Great,* by William M. Akers (Michael Wiese Productions, 2008); *The Writer's Guide to Writing Your Screenplay: How to Write Great Screenplays for Movies and Television,* by Cynthia Whitcomb (Kalmbach Publishing Co., 2002); *Save The Cat! The Last Book on Screenwriting You'll Ever Need,* by Blake Snyder (Michael Wiese Productions, 2005) These are just a few, but it's my hope they will turn on a light bulb or two for you.

Bare bones / Skeleton of any writing

# Flash Fiction 101

## *By S.D. Grimm*

**Fiction in a Flash**

In the simplest terms, flash fiction is a story in 1,000 words or less. Yep. A whole story—any genre—in less than approximately four double-spaced pages.

You might wonder it it's possible to write a story in under 1,000 words, and I'm here to tell you that it is. I've read flash fiction pieces in as little as six words before. If you think that's tough, consider micro fiction, a story in under 500 words; or nano fiction, a story in under 100 words or less.

But don't be discouraged. Once you understand the basics of how to write flash fiction, I think you'll want to try it out. Just be careful; writing flash fiction can be like eating potato chips—good luck stopping at just one.

**No Flash in the Pan**

Who doesn't love a good story? Remember sitting around the campfire or at a slumber party and staying up late to listen to ghost stories? People love stories, and sometimes, they don't want to read a huge novel or watch a two-hour movie. There is a whole audience out there of people who want to be able to read something on the go—on their mobile devices even.

There is an audience out there that is craving flash fiction.

Who can write flash fiction? You can!

As a flash fiction editor, I'm going to break down the fundamentals of what makes up "good" flash fiction for you and give you some tricks of the trade so you can write flash fiction.

**Ten Components of Good Flash Fiction**

**1. Structure**

Just like any narrative, flash fiction needs a beginning, middle, and end.

A clear story goal, a.k.a. plot.

Well-developed hero and villain, whether it's man vs man, man vs self, man vs nature, etc.

Setting

But unique to Flash Fiction:

You're not going to have subplots. There just isn't room in something so short. So focus on one plot and one main conflict. Conflict is the heart and soul of a story, and the main conflict needs to appear in a flash fiction piece pretty much immediately.

Another thing you don't want to overdo are scene changes and point-of-view switches. It can be done, and I've seen it done successfully, but when editing and rewriting, ask yourself if the change is really necessary. Often it will just complicate the plot in ways that don't enhance the story.

**2. Hook**

In a novel, the opening hook is that first scene that draws the reader into a new world. Many times flash fiction will play out its entire story in one scene. So the hook here is the opening sentence. It should set the tone for the story as well as introduce your reader to your character and give an inkling of the main conflict (if it doesn't delve right into the main conflict).

I've heard it said that novelists have 250 words to hook a reader. In flash, that's one quarter of a long story. Other stories might even be done already. You have to grab readers' attention in the opening line and never let go. If a reader puts down your flash piece, it's the death sentence.

**3. Tension**

It's that "what's going to happen next" factor. Great storytellers create tension in every scene. When you write flash fiction, there needs to be tension in every *sentence*. Each sentence needs to move the story forward. Imagine if you can craft a story in which you have tension in every line. Think of how that will improve your writing.

**4. Tight Writing**

Every word counts when you have so few. So here are a few tips for using words effectively:

Backload sentences. This means putting an important, resonating, or strong word or phrase at the end of a sentence. So instead of saying, "She noticed the dagger in his hand," try "He carried a dagger."

Use dynamic verbs. Tight writing forces you to rethink using those pesky verbs of being in exchange for something stronger, punchier. Instead of "broke" how about "shattered" or "snapped" or "crushed"? These different verbs each convey a more specific form of breakage that will make a reader's mental image sharper.

Pick specific nouns. Instead of "car" try "Volvo" or "Mustang." Or how about "Dachshund" in place of "dog"? Again, specific images are invoked.

Use adjectives and adverbs in their most powerful form: sparingly. Instead of a huge, puffy, white cloud, pick one. Or pick something different: a cotton-ball cloud.

Watch those passive-~~aggressive~~-voice sentences. They often require more words. By using strong verbs in active sentences, you will keep your word count low and the reader moving through the story.

Beware, though. Tight writing doesn't always mean you should choose the shortest possible sentences. Slipping into telling mode (instead of showing) for the sake of using less words isn't going to make the story strong. And be careful that you don't overload with adverbs for the sake of conciseness. You still have to SHOW your action, your emotion and your conflict. Flash isn't about sacrificing good writing for fewer words. It's an art all its own.

**5. Creative Title**

I've said every word counts, which includes titles. They don't count as part of your limited word count, but that doesn't mean it's a chance to get verbose. Pick something clever or that has a double meaning. Maybe the tile will be a red herring or give readers an extra tidbit about the story. Load your title with subtext whenever possible.

For example, I once wrote a flash piece titled *Fearfully and Wonderfully*. The theme of the story was about how everyone is different and beautiful in their own way. The plot was about the main character's death and how afraid she was, but that she ended up not needed to be so afraid because she wasn't alone—the person with her helped her find the beauty even in her passing. I thought the title played with both of those meanings.

Another example is a story titled *Mirror, Mirror*. Since it was a take on a retelling of the famous Snow White tale, the title helped readers make that connection before they even started reading.

Those kinds of hints can ground readers in context, or help the story resonate after they read it and the title brings extra meaning.

**6. Setting**

Every story needs a setting. It's easy to think that with a limited word count, setting is a throw away, but it's not. Readers need a sense of place and time and of who is in the room. Revert back to those deliberate nouns and pick and choose your adjectives carefully.

You can zero in on a specific part of the setting—like a vine crawling up a flagpole out of an abandoned playground's crumbled asphalt. Those are specific details that give a broad sense of setting: abandoned, new life, or possibly something choking life from something else. Imagery in setting is so full of subtext. Use that to your advantage in flash fiction when you can. And make your setting a character. Not just a place card for your characters.

**7. Character and POV**

As I mentioned earlier, you need a clear hero and villain. Just like in other forms of storytelling, you need to make sure your characters aren't boring, cookie-cutter, cardboard, people. Make them real. Breathe life into them.

In flash fiction, you want a small cast of characters. Large casts are warranted if you're writing in a genre like epic fantasy. Not in flash. You don't have time to introduce a huge cast and still have room for plot.

After you've settled on your short list of characters, choose your POV carefully. You'll probably only have one. Who will have the most to lose? The highest stakes? That's your POV character. And don't be afraid to think outside the box. I once wrote a piece in which the POV character was a snowflake.

**8. Backstory**

Every story has backstory. But the thing about backstory is that it already happened and doesn't need to be explained. Needed information should come out naturally in the story and only as the reader needs to know. You do not have time in your flash pieces to dump a bunch of BS (backstory, people!) at the beginning and then get on with your story. Flash forces you to weave in the things your reader needs to know organically.

**9. Emotional Investment**

All great fiction connects with readers on an emotional level. That's what they're looking for. Flash is no exception. This is why you need to *show* and not *tell* those emotional experiences. For example, not: "Harry gritted his teeth in determination." Instead, simply write: "Harry gritted his teeth." The context will let me know why, and what emotion he's feeling. Readers don't want to be told how to feel. They want to feel it with the character. Sometimes naming an emotion has its place, but showing the emotions builds a better connection with the readers. The limited word count of a Flash Fiction piece makes emotional investment even more imperative.

**10. Twist**

Unique to flash fiction is the twist ending. A lot of stories have a twist at the end, but it's always a part of flash fiction. You'd think it would make the story predictable, and that's where the fun of writing it comes in. The twist doesn't always happen at the end, but it should be near the end. It makes the end satisfying and hard-striking. The whole story leads up to that moment, and it's so perfectly set up and veiled at the same time. You're pulling the blindfold off the reader, but having them nod and say, "Yes! I—Yes, this is exactly how it should have been! I should have seen it coming!"

**Unleash Your Creativity**

Writing flash fiction is great for writers in general. Here are a few thoughts on why.

**1. Publishing Credit**

Flash Fiction stories are a real publishing credit. This looks great on query letters for those of you looking to eventually find and agent or publisher. I work for Splickety Publishing Group, and we publish a flash fiction magazine every month. That's twelve opportunities a year with just one venue. Get out there and see who publishes flash fiction.

**2. Promotional Materials/Freebies for Websites and Newsletters**

Readers want all kinds of extras, whether it's a unique original flash fiction piece, or a flash fiction piece that's in the story world of a longer piece you've written.

**3. Keeping Your Creative Muscles Strong**

Creativity is like a muscle. Keep using it and it keeps getting stronger. Sometimes when I'm between projects or waiting for one to sit while I stay away from editing it, I still want to keep that creativity muscle going. It's fabulous for helping that.

**4. The Satisfaction of Completing a Story**

Sometimes we writers work on a longer piece of fiction as well and when we do, we can work on something for months or even years before typing "the end." Then we have to go through the whole editing process. With flash fiction, you still have to write the piece and you still have to go through the editing process, but with 1000 words or less, the whole process is so much faster. At the end you have a complete story, and you're using your editing muscles. It's win/win.

What are you waiting for? Give it a try. Flex your creativity. Write on.

# *Fearfully and Wonderfully*

## *Flash Fiction by S.D. Grimm*

Everything is so cold. My arms splay unnaturally from my sides, brittle, like if I move they will shatter. I remember the rush of air against my body, pushing back as I dropped to the ground, and then the jolt as I slammed into the bed of snow.

I don't feel pain anymore. Just cold.

Pale light lifts over the mountaintops. Soon the sun will rise. Will I see it? Doubt fills my heart. I don't have long. Does he?

He held my hand the whole way down and told me not to fear, not to cry. Where is he? Icy chills run through my veins. I don't want to be alone.

Something delicate brushes against my arm and I turn my head, carefully.

His eyes, blue like a spruce, meet mine. "Are you afraid, little one?"

I smooth my hand over his, willing my body to move closer. It doesn't comply. "This is different than I thought it would be."

He smiles. "Don't worry. It's a journey we all must take."

"I'm glad you're here."

His eyes flash bright as he glances toward the rising sun.

A hint of warmth hits my body, softens the rigidness of my being. I relax. This is natural, as short as my life here has been. "It's almost time, isn't it?"

His eyes are wet. "You will be fine, little one. Trust me."

I envy him. He's always been so sure.

The wind is warmer now, just a touch. His delicate fingers trace the outline of my arm—so pale, white, and translucent. He always thought me beautiful, I don't know why, and he still looks at me with those same soft eyes.

I try again to inch closer to no avail. "How do you know so much?"

"Don't you think *he* will care for you?"

The worry in me grows. "Why should he? I am flawed and—"

"He made you. No one will ever look like you, be like you. That's how much he cares. You are intricate, unique, original. Even now you are no less beautiful."

He touches my shattered arm again and I flinch. Not because it hurts. Nothing hurts anymore. It's too warm for that. I'm just now understanding.

How much time had I wasted worrying about my imperfections? He sees past them. I'm the only one who doesn't.

The blanket of white beneath me sparkles. Each snowflake does its part to make the whole winter world shine. When we are together no individual snowflake's flaws stand out. Together, we compensate for one another's weaknesses.

Warmth settles in my chest. Wetness blurs my vision.

"I will go with you, if you like, little one," he whispers.

He wanted me to see all the beauty there was to see in life. And now in death.

Light glares above. I can no longer feel his hand. I don't even know if I'm still holding on to him. Heat envelops me. I feel my body no longer. All my joints turn to water. These are my last moments.

I open my mouth, afraid I won't be able to speak once I've melted. "When we meet our maker, will it be cold there?"

His smile is the same, but his face is different. It's not a face I've seen before, but I know I am staring at my maker, at Father Frost himself.

Those unmistakable blue-spruce eyes send one last comforting shiver through me. "Yes, little snowflake. It will be very cold there."[14]

14 First published in *Splickety Magazine*, 2.3, December, 2013.

# *Why Poetry? Reading and Writing Poetry in a World of Prose*

*By Matthew Landrum*

Late sun poured across the college, casting the fielders' long shadows across the common lawn. The annual poets versus prose softball game was tied at the bottom of the thirteenth inning and I was up to bat. I squinted against the level light and heard the satisfying crack of softball on wood. I managed a double. The novelist on second base pounded his glove as we waited for the next hit. A strike and then a single. I ran and got tagged out. Two outs. The essayist catcher was reciting "Casey at the Bat" as I made my way back to the sidelines, *there was no joy in Mudville, mighty Casey had struck out*. But the next hit was true. A solid hit. The baserunner rounded third while the ball was relayed from the far outfield. The game was over.

The Bennington College annual softball match pits poets against prose writers—all fun and games. But the view that poets and prose are opposing sides extends well beyond the softball field. Ask about genre at a writer's conference and most will split one way or another. *I write poetry. I'm working on a memoir. I'm finishing my second novel.* Most poets read novels and personal essays but many prose writers don't read poetry, thinking it hard or irrelevant. And it can be those things, in the same way much of the fiction at Barnes & Noble isn't worth reading. But poetry has so much to offer any writer. Any prose writer not reading (and even trying their hand at writing) poetry is missing out on what it has to offer their craft.

At every conference where I speak, I get asked what the difference between poetry and prose is. One common assumption is that poetry rhymes and prose doesn't. But that's not it and it's more complicated than that. After talking myself in circles the first few times this conversation came up, I developed this answer: *Poetry is the intentional use of language, its every trick and tool to create meaning. Prose is usually concerned with information.* The extra layers of meaning in poetry are why it's so important for writers to take it in as part of their regular diet of reading.

**Musicality**

When I was in my teens and early twenties, I wanted nothing more in the world than to be a rocker. I wrote songs, played shows and played in bands. After three years with a band in college, I found myself falling out of love with that dream. Playing show after show, repeating the same eight or ten songs, took all the fun out of music. I wanted to create. I traded that pursuit in for writing. And to my surprise, I found it a better fit for my love of music than guitar ever was.

It might seem counter-intuitive that writing poetry could be a better fit for a musician than playing music, but there are few things more musical than writing. Words flow. They rise. They fall. They come out slow or pattern in rapid fire. They are music. Even on the page. Poets in the 17th century talk about their poems as songs. Because they are. In this information age, it's easy to forget that words convey meaning beyond their dictionary definition. But we all know that a simple tone change can turn a compliment into a sarcastic jab. That a change in pitch at a sentence's end can turn a statement into a question. That's music.

When authors own the musicality of language, they unlock an additional level of meaning they can use to reach their readers. Take Roethke's "My Papa's Waltz" about cavorting around the kitchen with his drunken dad.

*The whiskey on your breath*
*Could make a small boy dizzy;*
*But I hung on like death:*
*Such waltzing was not easy.* [15]

The rhythm flails and two steps and keeps time to the drunken waltz of the poem. It accentuates the meaning.

Musicality can also counter meaning as in Wendy Cope's "Lonely Hearts," a rhyming metrical poem based on personal ads from the London papers.

*Can someone make my simple wish come true?*
*Male biker seeks female for touring fun.*
*Do you live in North London? Is it you?*
*Gay vegetarian whose friends are few,*

---

15 https://www.poetryfoundation.org/poems-and-poets/poems/detail/43330 accessed May 17, 2017

*I'm into music, Shakespeare, and the sun.*
*Can someone make my simple wish come true?*[16]

It feels like a nursery rhyme. Lulled along on the music, I almost forget what a sad poem it is. Loneliness persists. Desperate people adopt desperate measures. The music is happy. The words are sad. The two currents sweep in opposite directions, swirling into a riptide of meaning that pulls me down more effectively than either could do on their own.

**Word Choice**

I read an interview with a translator who, as a student, had been fired from a translation project for using the word *turquoise* to describe the color of a flower. The head of the project told her to pack her things, that anyone who described a flower with a stone shouldn't be working on poetry. I've never experienced such a harsh view of language but working as a translator, I've come across some moments where word choice matters.

I was translating a poem by Jóanes Nielsen in which a flirtatious poet is making eyes at a woman. My co-translator translated one line as, "he had the gleam of a predator in his eyes." To a Faroese speaker, predator means an animal that hunts. In America, it has all sorts of nasty connotations—I think of the television show "To Catch a Predator." I rendered the final as "wolf."

It's easy to think of examples of word choice affecting meaning. Think of words that have the same dictionary definition—forest and woods, village and town, beach and seashore. Though they may mean the same thing, they have different connotations and cultural weights. To me a rock and a stone are different things.

Science backs this up. A 2001 experiment had speakers of Spanish, Tamil, and English assign the names Bouba and Kiki to the shapes below.[17]

16 http://writersalmanac.publicradio.org/index.php?date=2001/12/06 accessed May 17, 2017

17 https://www.theguardian.com/science/head-quarters/2016/oct/17/the-boubakiki-effect-how-do-we-link-shapes-to-sounds accessed May 17, 2017

Overwhelmingly, people assigned Kiki to the first figure and Bouba to the second. The implications of the so called Bouba/Kiki effect? The sounds of words and how they feel in the mount creates meaning.

I know I get excited when I find the perfect word. I think most writers can relate to that. Poetry can help hone the awareness of word choice.

**The Leap**

Writing can be dangerous. I know I've had to restrain myself from reaching for my notebook when I'm driving and a cedar-sided house makes me think of islands in the Baltic or level sunlight blinding me to the road forcibly recalls hazy childhood summers. This is common for writers. We write all the time, even when we're nowhere near a pen or keyboard. One minute we're gardening and then the feel of the rake's smoothed wood handle suddenly leads to an epiphany and we run inside, tracking dirt, to jot down a paragraph. It makes us hard to live with. But really, one thing leading to something completely different is human. We're non-linear, associative thinkers.

I call the jump from one thing to another the leap. A traveler stops his horse by a snow-filled forest and thinks of the great weariness of human life. Grammar practice gives way to the idea that love should be expressed without rules. This is the leap. Poetry is perfect for it.

One of my favorite leaps is in "Love Calls Us to the Things of This World" by Richard Wilbur. A man wakes up as a clothesline pulley is winched between buildings and sees, in the groggy moments before properly waking, the billowing blouses and dresses as angels of air.

*Outside the open window*
*The morning air is all awash with angels.*
*Some are in bed-sheets, some are in blouses,*
*Some are in smocks: but truly there they are.*
*Now they are rising together in calm swells*
*Of halcyon feeling, filling whatever they wear*
*With the deep joy of their impersonal breathing;*
*Reality intrudes and the day comes but the man is left with an epiphany.*
*Yet, as the sun acknowledges*
*With a warm look the world's hunks and colors,*
*The soul descends once more in bitter love*
*To accept the waking body, saying now*
*In a changed voice as the man yawns and rises,*

*"Bring them down from their ruddy gallows;*
*Let there be clean linen for the backs of thieves;*
*Let lovers go fresh and sweet to be undone,*
*And the heaviest nuns walk in a pure floating*
*Of dark habits,*
*keeping their difficult balance."*[18]

That's the leap! Going from laundry to a mantra for life. It is the beating heart of poetry but is by no means special to poetry. Novelists, essayists, and memoirists can and should take the leap and use rhythm to make the reader dance and use word choice to bring their work to life. Poets and prose writers are not on different teams. They're on the same team, the team of loving words and seeking meaning and truth in text. Rather than opponents, they're specialists in different areas and they have so much to offer each other.

I've learned so much from the novelists and short-story writers in my writers' group. But that's a different essay. Try a few books of poetry. Even try writing if you feel the urge. Whether reading or writing, just have fun on the page. Don't worry about perfect understanding or execution. Let the music carry you.

**Where to Begin**

My day job—if talking about your favorite things all day can really be considered work—is teaching high school. A good number of my students love poetry or come to love poetry but many of them enter my class with myths and misconceptions. They think poetry is hard. They think they're too dumb to understand it and wonder why anyone would bother anyway. But these kids were children once and children love poetry. Think of the playground rhymes for jump-rope or nursery rhymes—poetry is natural to kids. Jaded high school students had to learn to dislike poetry and they learned it from a society that doesn't like or read poetry. Writers aren't immune to this influence.

One reason for this is that in the Sixties onward for the next 30 years, poetry got weird. Academics and beat poets made poetry that was intentionally difficult, navel-gazing and odd, and insulted people for liking more traditional, relatable verse. There's been a resurgence in accessible poetry in

---

18 https://www.poetryfoundation.org/poems-and-poets/poems/detail/43048.

the last few decades but society still thinks of poetry as overly specialized and no fun.

A few years back, my dad made a new year's resolution to find new music. "I've been listening to the same stuff since high school," he said. And he had. He asked his Facebook friends to recommend a CD. Next time I visited home, he had Fleet Foxes, The Killers, and Drake sitting on the counter. He professes to like it all.

Starting off with poetry blindly would be like walking into a record shop, picking a random CD and purchasing it. Chances are you wouldn't like it. Just like music, poetry has genres. There are different styles and voices and subject matter. Not liking some poetry doesn't equate to not liking all poetry. Try some out. See what happens. Here are few recommendations.

Li-Young Lee, *The City in Which I Love You* (BOA Editions Ltd., 1990)—This is a perfect book for romantics. It's about marriage, love, immigration, faith, and creating a family.

Louise Glück, *The Wild Iris* (Ecco reprint edition, 2993)—Glück takes the leap in the book about flowers. Moving from perennial bulbs to resurrection, from blooms to the afterlife, this is a book about religion as much as about gardening.

Claudia Emerson, *Late Wife: Poems* (LSU Press, 2005)—Poetry works as an act of moving on as a post-divorce woman confronts singleness and memory in the former-marriage house.

Franz Wright, *Walking to Martha's Vineyard: Poems* (Knopf reprint edition, 2005)—This book is an exuberant movement toward faith out of the shadows of mental illness and drug abuse. Its hopeful belief that even the damaged can be made whole is paired with a fragmental, short style.

Seamus Heaney, *The Spirit Level* (Farrar, Straus and Giroux reprint edition, 1997)—The greatest poet of the last 30 years, the late Heaney brings his art to a perfect pitch in this book. He examines common objects (a rainstick, a level) and finds deep meaning in them.

A.E. Stallings, *Olives: Poems* (TriQuarterly Books, 2012)—This rhyming metrical book talks about fairy tales, love and religion in a fresh and contemporary way.

Paul Muldoon, *Horse Latitudes: Poems* (Farrar, Straus and Giroux, 2007)—For lovers of music, this former poetry editor of *The New Yorker* takes us on a punk-rock approach to language, which is a joy to read aloud.

Rebecca Lindenberg, *Love, an Index* (McSweeney's, 2012)—This book mixes mourning with Facebook posts as the author grieves for her long-term boyfriend who died hiking on a volcano.

Michael Robbins, *Alien vs. Predator* (Penguin Books, 2012)—Pop-culture references get mixed and remixed in a book of singsong poetry about real issues in American culture.

Poetry can be about anything. It doesn't have to rhyme or be fancy or immediately profound. Try starting by describing things. Keep it simple. Have fun. It's how I write best. I'll leave you with one of my poems that came out of describing coffee and chess with a friend.

A CHESSBOARD IN SUNLIGHT
*for Fredrik Ek Sotka*

*Afternoon sunlight through the café patio's hothouse glass*
*throws black and white into sharper relief, raises the temperature*
*to indoor summer in spite of the cold Atlantic wind. Our sweaters*
*and jackets*
*lie draped over chair backs. A bee flits from cup to cup, sipping at dregs*
*of red wine and sweetened coffee. With a handful of pawns and*
*minor nobility*
*taken on either side, the game is close to even, still in its early stages.*
*Beyond the glass, wind ruffles the surface of the harbor, snatches at the flag*
*over the parliamentary house. Tomorrow, I take the first bus to the airport.*
*Knight to pawn four, queen to bishop six—one decision will be answered*
*by another*
*and a path will open in the future's checkered expanse. There are so many*
*possibilities.*
*Two pawns down for black and now it's your move.*

# One in a Thousand, One of a Thousand: Finding a Place in Literary Journals

*By John Winkelman*

Back in 1993 I landed my dream job at a big independent bookstore in Grand Rapids, Michigan. After six years of college I had finally graduated and was working as a prep cook, and feeling somewhat at loose ends. The bookstore job felt like a return home. I was surrounded by creative readers who themselves were not ready to make the transition to the real world—whatever that was. This was back in the days before Amazon, when books were discovered by reading other books, and rare works by favorite authors were hard to come by, and sometimes existed as little more than rumor.

On the rare occasion when a new collection of short fiction or poetry by Jim Harrison or Denise Levertov or Michael Swanwick hit the shelves, I would become a hermit for a weekend and devour the work cover to cover. But at the end I was always left with the feeling I was standing just outside the door of a club full of the most interesting people in the world. These collections were glimpses, and sometimes years out of date, with years to wait until the next one.

After some time I began to notice the notes accompanying the works in the collections—lists of the venues where the stories, essays and poems had originally been printed. These were publications with powerful and compelling titles like *Salmagundi* and *The Paris Review*, *Omni* and *Zyzzyva*, *Glimmer Train* and *Azimov's*.

These weren't magazines—these were *journals*! These were publications with *gravitas*, worthy of respect. These were places a feckless young twenty-something might make his bones as a writer. And they were right there, on the other side of that door.

So I did what anyone would do when facing a closed door: I began shoving things through the mail slot. In hindsight, I wasn't very professional about it. I would have an idea on Friday, spend Saturday and Sunday banging out a two thousand word lump of Lovecraftian horror, and send it off in the mail on the way to work on Monday. This was back in the days when few magazines had an online presence, and almost nobody accepted work by email. A standard submission was the work, printed double-spaced and stapled, in a large envelope which also contained a self-addressed, stamped envelope in which would be returned the publisher's response. For me, 100 percent of the time it was a rejection letter. Most of them were form letters containing variations on "try again." I think I received exactly one personalized rejection, and that magazine went out of business the next year.

Working at the bookstore, I was surrounded by people who had similar stories, though they generally had better luck than I did, mostly because they edited their work and ran it by other people before sending it out into the wild. I didn't have time for all that. I was too busy trying to get published!

This pattern of writing and receiving rejections continued for a few years, and eventually life took me in other directions.

Fast forward to early 2015. Caffeinated Press had been in business for a few months and we were looking for a way to expand our offering. To paraphrase Captain Willard in *Apocalypse Now*, I wanted a literary journal, and for my sins, they gave me one.

*The 3288 Review* started slow, as all new ventures do, but quickly ramped up as we gained presence in large online resources like *Poets & Writers, Duotrope* and *NewPages*. A handful of submissions a month quickly became a handful of submissions a day, finally leveling off at an average of 900 submissions a year—quite remarkable for a brand-new quarterly literary journal with a small regional focus. We found ourselves spending hours every day reading, voting, editing, designing, writing acceptance and rejection letters, cutting checks, and driving to the post office. Running a literary journal, it turns out, is a lot of work.

Many of our submissions came from writers who owned or worked for other literary journals. I talked to several of them and they all agreed that yes, publishing is a lot of work. The budgets are miniscule, the pay even smaller, and the time commitment crowds out all but the most important of other daily considerations. They also agreed that there are never enough people available for the work that needs to be done. Editing is mentally and emotionally demanding work, and with so little money available it can be difficult to find people to fill the necessary roles. It was only through the strict time management and sleep deprivation that they had been able to create the work they had submitted to us.

So of course I had to ask: "Is it worth it?" The answer was a unanimous "ABSOLUTELY!" Literary magazines are at the leading edge of the publishing world. Thousands of editors at thousands of venues read thousands of submissions a month, polishing and curating the work and showcasing it to the world at large. The work that crosses our desks could be the first poem a young writer has ever submitted for consideration, or the finely-tuned masterpiece of a world-class wordsmith. A volunteer editor or college intern might be the first person to read an essay which goes on to win the Pushcart Prize or a Pulitzer.

Those numbers are not an exaggeration. There are well over a thousand literary and genre magazines in the United States, and many times that number worldwide. And for each venue there are often more than a thousand submissions a year waiting to be read, out of which at most one percent will see publication. For every work by Ocean Vuong, there are a hundred worthy poems which must be turned down because of space or scheduling constraints or because they don't quite fit the venue. For every story by James Salter, there are innumerable others which will be rejected for simple line editing errors or misspellings.

So there it is: a thousand venues per writer, and a thousand writers per venue. It is no exaggeration to say more than a million submissions are vetted in a given year. The biggest challenge to getting published is not a lack of outlets, but finding the right one, and distinguishing yourself from the crowd.

The following list contains suggestions to help writers (and artists!) fine-tune their submissions to journals and magazines. The suggestions apply to literary and genre publications, in both print and online venues.

These suggestions assume that you have already thoroughly edited your work, had someone else read it, made edits based on feedback from these beta readers, and so on. If this due diligence has not yet happened, then you are not yet ready to submit your work for publication.

**Research Before You Submit**

With more than a thousand literary journals out there, it is a good idea to spend some time making lists of the venues that best match your creative work. Journals come in all shapes and sizes, and conform to myriad design and editorial standards. More importantly, and more difficult to define, each journal has its own "feel," which is the standard by which the readers and editors judge fitness of a piece for publication. Spend some time in the stacks at a library or bookstore. If you have a favorite writer, one whose writing you feel is similar to your own, find out where that person has been published. It may not be a perfect fit, but it is a good place to start. Compare what you have written to what the journals publish, and ask yourself: Is my work a good example of this sort of thing?

**Read the Submission Guidelines**

Just as every journal has its own voice, every journal has its own list of submission guidelines. Some are quite simple, like "Please include your email address." Some are lengthy, with a score or more of rules by which a submission must abide. While those guidelines may all look alike at first glance, it is the little differences which can direct your submission into the reject pile. For example: many journals require that your submission be in the form of a Word document or PDF which has been anonymized. This means the document should not have any personal information on it, anywhere. Not in the body of the text, not in the document header or footer, and not in the filename of the document. This is a standard enough practice that it seldom requires a second glance. On the other end, there could be a format requirement so specific that it only appears in one journal in a hundred. If the journal says "minimum 1,000 words," and your story is 990 words, then that journal is not the right venue for your work. If you find yourself compelled to add a note saying "I know you normally don't publish things like this, but..." then this is not the right venue for your work.

**Have Someone Else Read Your Work Before You Submit It**

Craft is one thing, but the more nebulous qualities which make a good story a great story are harder to judge. A good reader can tell you if your dialogue sounds realistic; if the narrative voice is internally consistent; if the events depicted could fit inside the timeline of the story. For poetry, workshopping can strengthen language and allow exploration of metaphors and wordplay which might not be apparent to the poet.

**Read (and Preferably Purchase) a Recent Copy of Any Journal to Which You Will Submit**

The best way to determine if your work is a good fit for a magazine is to read that magazine. And the best way to support a magazine—and help ensure it remains in business to publish your work—is to give them a little money in return for some excellent writing. This may sound counter-intuitive if you place a lot of importance on being compensated for your work, but consider: a single issue likely costs less than the compensation you will receive from a paying market, and reading that magazine will help determine if it is a good fit for you. And if it isn't a good fit for a piece you have ready to submit, then it might open doors and pathways to a future work which you can then send on, having already done your research.

**Be Persistent**

Rejection is inevitable and unavoidable. It is also part of the process of being published. When you receive a rejection letter, mark it off on your spreadsheet and send your work to another journal. Or wait a year and send it to the same journal again. There may be new readers and editors, and perhaps this time your poem will resonate with someone where it didn't before. The most successful writers and artists are the ones who work at it, day in and day out. We have had poets send their work to us half a dozen times before we published them. They kept at it through a year and a half of rejection slips before the right pair of eyes saw the right poems at the right time.

**Be Patient**

Remember the part about journals being understaffed? Scale your expectations to months and years, not days and weeks. If a venue says they will respond within 90 days, do not expect a response until the 90th day. A good rule of thumb is to expect a response in about 150 percent of the time suggested in the editorial guidelines. Life happens. People have children. Interns get sick. Servers crash. For instance, in autumn 2016 we discovered that our email server had been added to a list of known sources of spam. By the time the situation was resolved, 90 days had come and gone on many of our submissions.

Also be patient with yourself. If a publication deadline looms and your piece is not yet ready to release into the wild, keep working on it. Better to wait three or six months for the next submission window than to let something go before you have polished it to perfection.

**Be Professional**

Don't take rejection personally. Don't take editorial suggestions personally. Keep careful track of your submissions, your acceptances and rejections. Realize that while writing is an art, being published is as much a business as being a publisher. I have talked to poets who keep large spreadsheets of their poetry submissions, sometimes going back 15 or 20 years. They keep records of every interaction with every publisher who has ever read their work. At the beginning this may seem like a lot of extra effort for very little gain, but the value of being able to easily review the status and history of your collected work cannot be overstated. And in the event you are successful enough at your trade that the IRS takes notice, you will be glad for the extra time spent.

**And Finally:**
Never, *ever* stop creating.

# See What Happens: Writing Your First Picture Book

*By Kenneth Kraegel*

I am always interested to hear how other artists go about their work. I like to know where they work, when they work, what their routine is, all of that. I have this ideal in my mind of how the lives of writers are supposed to be. They live in beautiful old houses that are in walking distance to funky, vibrant urban centers, yet are somehow also located in secluded picturesque rural settings with old barns, giant maples and stone fences that have been standing for 200 years. When they are ready to write, they sit down in pristine, naturally lit rooms with walls that are full of neatly shelved books. A bit of ivy taps lightly at one of the many windows. They are perfectly dressed for the occasion, in simple, comfortable-looking clothes, but on second glance, they look kind of sexy too. They take a careful sip of coffee and begin. These people write brilliant stuff for a few hours, taking breaks to step into their tastefully updated kitchens for a refill of coffee and to let the sweet old family dog out. (What is name of the dog? Euripides? Auden? Or maybe Buster, so as not to be too pretentious.) Eventually they receive phone calls from excited editors and publicists who can't wait to tell them really good news.

**The Real Beans**

My actual process for writing picture books isn't like that at all, although I do sometimes drink coffee while I work and there is one maple tree between my house and the street. Do I ever look sexy? I wonder. Regardless, writing picture books is still a pretty exciting journey.

For me, the very beginning of a book starts with a story idea or just the desire to make something. Either way, I force myself to make three finished illustrations before I do any writing. If I don't have an idea for a story, I just start drawing a tree or something and eventually an idea for a story emerges. These pictures take me around six weeks to complete and having that extra time before actually writing the story seems to be important for developing it in my mind. Since, while I am working on those first three pictures my focus is mainly on the drawing and painting, my mind can circle leisurely around the story without needing to come up with something immediately. By the time I have finished the three illustrations, I have had enough low-pressure time to develop a basic story idea. Those three finished illustrations sometimes stay central to the story and other times they end up as sample illustrations that I include with my proposal, but either way, they give my imagination time to percolate and are therefore worth the effort.

**Figure 1.** *One of the three finished illustrations that I made before I wrote* Green Pants. *It ended up being very similar to the one used in the book.*

After I have completed the three illustrations, I begin writing the story. Since I am also the illustrator of my stories, I use a storyboard, writing and sketching each page before I move on to the next. I make my sketches on paper and scan them into Photoshop where I drop them into a storyboard and add the text. This is the ugly part of the process where all the writing and rewriting takes place. You could call it the first draft. Like underwear, the first draft is essential, but you are not required to show it to anyone and most people would rather you didn't. In this stage a lot of experimentation happens, which is part of what makes the process messy, but also how I find the right direction. Before I add a new page to the storyboard, I reread the previous pages and rework them, so by the time I have reached the last page, the first pages have been revised many times. I continue wrestling with the story, working out any problems I see until it seems to be as coherent and meaningful as I can make it.

I then repackage the words and sketches into a book dummy. A few years ago the dummy was an actual paper mockup of the proposed book with the text and sketches laid out together on each page. Now I lay the pages out in Photoshop and then send them to my editor as a multi-page PDF.

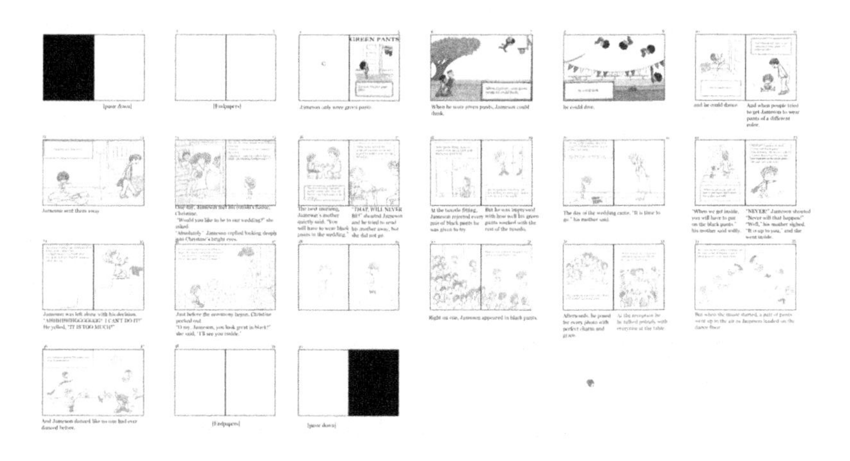

**Figure 2.** *The storyboard for* Green Pants. *This is where all the work takes place.*

*Fig. 1-3 in this chapter are copyright 2017 by Kenneth Kraegel. Reproduced by permission of the publisher, Candleick Press, Somerville, MA.*

**Tips for Writing a Picture Book**

So that is how I write a picture book, but everyone will do it differently. Below are a few things that might be helpful to know.

The word count of picture books varies quite a bit. The typical word count for fiction picture books probably falls into the zero-to-1,200 range, but there may be good reasons for a longer word count. The illustrations in a picture book do a lot of the storytelling, so the text for a picture book should be on the lean side. You don't need to say, "*Phillip was looking glum because his shoelace had broken. He wanted to cry, but held it in.*" All you need is, "*Phillip wanted to cry,*" and everything else will be conveyed by the illustration. Don't get too bogged down by analyzing what can and can't be conveyed by the illustration, just go with what seems right to you.

In your manuscript, if you want to indicate something that should be conveyed by the illustration, it is usually acceptable to put a brief illustration note in brackets. However, you should only include illustration notes that are essential to the reader's understanding of the story. It will be up to the illustrator, in consultation with the art director and editor, to determine what each illustration should look like. If you are the author *and* the illustrator, you should submit a book dummy instead of a manuscript and your combined words and sketches should contain everything essential to telling the story.

**Figure 3.** *A two-page spread from the book dummy proposal for* Green Pants.

For books created by a separate author and illustrator, the editor and art director will choose the illustrator. They will not expect the author to find an illustrator or even have much to say about how the pictures should look. They may take suggestions from the author and they may ask the author for her opinion of an illustrator's work, but in most cases, the publisher has the last word on who illustrates a book. People are often surprised to hear that the author and illustrator of a book are typically not in direct communication with each other but instead communicate only with the editor and art director. Usually an illustrator begins illustrating after the text is in its final, fully-edited and approved state. This arrangement can be disconcerting for the author since she is relinquishing some control of the vision that she had for the book. And, of course, there is the chance that the author will not like the illustrations, but that is not too common, since it is the goal of everyone involved to make the book as appealing as it can be.

The number of pages for picture books comes in multiples of eight with 32 and 40 pages being the most common. Authors don't really need to worry about this, nor do they need to worry about where the page breaks should fall. The editor and art director, in conversation with the illustrator, will work these issues out. There are a lot of different ways to design a picture book and the editor and art director will have good instincts for what will work the best for each project. For instance, I submitted my first book as a 32 page dummy and my editor and art director thought it worked better as a 40 page book—it did. Watching the design of the book evolve is so exciting. It is amazing to see what a polished product can emerge from the initial scratches on paper.

One thing to keep in mind when writing picture books is that they are meant to be performed—read aloud. Picture books are read aloud in some of the sweetest settings, on laps before bedtime or to a classroom full of eager, squirmy kids. There may be opportunities when you are writing your story to structure a sentence that includes subtle but useful stage directions. For instance, you could write: *"Man, that sandwich really really stinks!" Zoey whispered to herself.* But the reader won't read *"whispered"* (the stage direction) until after Zoey's statement was finished and so wouldn't know to whisper that sentence. This sentence is easy to change around so that the stage directions come earlier in the sentence, and give the reader a chance to whisper most of the sentence: *"Man," Zoey whispered to herself, "that sandwich really really stinks!"* And you may find other ways to add stage directions. SUCH AS ALL CAPS IF SOMEONE IS SPEAKING LOUDLY. OR, MY FAVORITE, ALL CAPS AND

**EXTRA LARGE TYPE**

FOR THOSE PIVOTAL MOMENTS WHEN SOMEONE IS REALLY YELLING! Letting the reader know how to read the book makes the book more fun to read aloud.

There is a push and pull within children's literature. Some expect that literature for children should be either educational or morally instructive. Others believe that readers will intuitively find in stories the inspiration that they need, and so it is not necessary for the writer to have a specific aim in mind. I feel both sides of that tension within me as I work on a story. I want my story to contain something meaningful to the reader, but I don't want the story to be preachy or awkwardly didactic. I do not write a story with a moral in mind, instead I try to write the best story that I can write and I follow the characters in their particular situation as honestly as I can. I trust that something worthwhile will rise to the surface if I follow that direction.

However, it could be that your sole purpose in writing a particular story is to teach a specific lesson. In that case you want to do it as artfully as possible, so that the complexity and poignancy of the lesson is conveyed within an engaging story. You don't want the reader to feel they are being taught a lesson, instead you want to draw them into an interesting story. Dr. Seuss is an obvious example. Some of his books have a very definite lesson behind them, but they are placed in such wild and interesting stories that the reader is happy to be along for the ride.

Eventually you will show your story, your beloved work-in-progress, to somebody and get some feedback. It can be tough to receive criticism, especially when you have considered every word and deliberated over every sentence! But, feedback is how you move forward. Please don't throw anything at the person who was kind enough to give you the feedback and don't send a knee-jerk, embarrassing email. Just be grateful and professional. Then, take some time to consider the critique before reacting to it. It usually takes me three or four readings of my editor's notes, over as many days, before I am able to wrap my mind around her comments and really know what to do with them. And, of course, not every critique you receive is a useful one. Or maybe I should say that a bad critique is only useful in helping you know which way you *don't* want to go.

**Do your Best, Then See What Happens**

I spent a lot of time wanting to be a picture book writer and illustrator before I actually started trying. On the one hand I thought I was brilliant, capable of amazing literary prowess, destined to be ranked up there with Shakespeare and T.S. Eliot (who I hadn't read). I was the chosen one who would take the picture book genre to dizzying new heights. On the other hand I was completely intimidated at the task of getting a book published or even of letting someone critique my work. So instead of giving the picture book dream a sustained effort, I dabbled in it occasionally and spent a lot of time lying on the couch wondering when someone would discover me. I think I was hoping an editor would be in a coffee shop getting some coffee when she would, out of the corner of her eye, happen to notice a peculiar and disarming intelligence on my face. She would surreptitiously look over my shoulder and read a poem that I had scrawled on a napkin. That was all it would take. There and then she would take me out to an expensive dinner, offer me a contract and beg me to take it.

That never happened.

After many years of thinking and dabbling, I finally gave it an earnest try. I worked regularly on my stories, attended conferences and put my work out where people could see it. Eventually I got some traction. I would guess that most writers fluctuate between over-confidence and low-confidence. Now I just keep at it, rain or shine. You can do this too. Just do the hard work, let it go and see what happens.

# Cartooning: A Journey from Dreaming to Doing

*By Samuel Carbaugh*

**Being One Who Makes Comics**

It's as difficult to define being a cartoonist as it is to define being a writer. What makes one a writer? By definition, one who writes *is* a writer. Therefore, one who creates a two-dimensional story not bound by time using words and images is a cartoonist. I'd wager that doesn't help you understand *how* to be one.

The only way I can tell you how to become a working cartoonist is via my own story. I'm no Charles Schulz and I haven't made a comic that has been adapted into a movie, but I have been able to make a modest living. It can be done. The future of comics is bright with our current media culture in love with stories, images and creative points of view. Cartooning is no longer narrowly defined as a comic strip in a newspaper or superheroes in flashy costumes. Cartooning exists in user manuals, textbooks, websites, documentaries, VR experiences and more. You have many more opportunities to make a living through cartooning than those a generation ago.

Ten years ago I didn't know how to start along the path I am walking now. I knew nothing of the wider world of cartooning and I knew even less about the actual craft. If you are like me, then you want someone to lay out the basic tips to get started. I hope what I can offer you will be of great help.

Everyone has his or her own path and you don't need to make a living at comics to be considered successful and respected. Drawing comics about your daily life and sharing them on social media can land you readers and accolades and open doors to other creative opportunities. The truth is the cartooning world is bigger now than at any time in the 20th century and your audience is out there.

**My Beginning, Your Beginning**

Garfield was my favorite thing in the world when I was 11. I watched the animated show, obsessively. I read the collected *Garfield* comics hundreds of times. I marveled at how the art and storytelling evolved from the late 1970s to the mid 1990s. I loved the jokes. Before I fell in love with comic books a year later, I knew I wanted to be a cartoonist.

I didn't stop to think if I had talent or not. Charles Schulz of *Peanuts* fame once said, "Cartooning is 99 percent hard work and 1 percent talent." I knew I loved the medium. I loved Garfield. So, I copied *Garfield* comics in notebooks. I made my own version of *Garfield*. Instead of a fat cat, I imagined an overweight bird. He hated Thursdays, not Mondays. He loved manicotti, not lasagna. The dumb animal he lived with wasn't a dog, it was a cat. I made strip after strip of this bird. I filled binders with hand-made parodies of movie posters that I called "Parroties" with amazing names like "Jurassic Lark" and "Fist Full of Feathers." None of those comics or posters would ever be seen published in a newspaper, but they taught me many lessons and gave me the hunger to dig deeper into how to make comics.

If you want to make comics, the first thing you need to do, is *make comics*. They won't be perfect, but you will learn far more by copying the style of your favorite cartoonist than just wishing you were an amazing artist. Find someone you love and copy their style. It's the best way to get started.

Cartooning is no different than playing a musical instrument. Hear me out. You may want to play Chopin someday on a baby grand piano, but if you are starting to learn you have to do what everyone else has done before you. Learn the basics. Find middle C. Play "Mary Had a Little Lamb" hundreds of times. Play "Chopsticks." Slowly learn more and more complicated pieces. You learn through repetition, practice and playing someone else's music.

Cartooning is the same way. Find a cartoonist whose style you love; if it's too complex, find a simpler example. Practice drawing various hands and faces for hours and hours. Practice lettering by hand. Draw characters again and again and again. Fill the margins of your notebooks with faces. Before you can create your own unique comic, you must first learn by copying.

But how to copy well? Kevin Huizenga, a cartoonist working in the literary graphic novel genre, told me his method and I still use it. If you like the way a certain cartoonist draws a tree, for example, copy the tree in your sketchbook while you look at the original drawing. Then, without looking at the original, copy your copy, twice. Finally, try drawing the tree on another sketchbook page without looking at your copies or the original. It's like mental magic. This process helps you internalize the techniques used by other cartoonists. Don't worry about being a fraud. If you are learning from multiple cartoonists then your work won't look like a copy, so much as your own piece of work influenced by other masters.

Just like music. Or poetry. Or any other creative action. Skills are learned through practice and copying masters.

My own cartooning style has evolved a great deal over the years. I've found the comics masters I admire and am still learning from their techniques. Jim Davis and his fat cat was only the beginning of my journey. Who is your Mr. Davis?

**Cartooning 101**

Comics creation, a.k.a. *Cartooning,* takes little more than a piece of paper and some drawing instruments. It can be as easy or complicated as you want to make it. Some cartoonists stick to the basics: paper, pencil, ink, scan, done. Some go deeper: various papers, multiple pencils, different inking styles, different inks, watercolors, acrylics, glitter, scan, edit digitally, print on different paper, rescan, etc. Others do everything from start to finish on the computer without ever picking up an inky pen. You will find your medium of choice in time. However, most cartoonists follow the same rough process when making comics.

A comic begins with an idea. Ideas need to be processed and analyzed. Cartoonists use thumbnails to help work out ideas on paper. A thumbnail is a micro version of the comic you want to make. The name comes from their smallish size, usually no larger than a literal thumbnail. Panels are tiny. Characters are micro stick figures. Dialogue is noted by a number and written outside the thumbnail. Thumbnails are excellent for working out comic ideas because they can be drawn in less than 10 seconds and if you hate an idea or panel structure and need to start again, just redraw the thumbnail.

Comics, whether Web, strip, or book, usually have panels. It's mostly how action and time are represented. For example a comic strip: Panel A sets the scene, Panel B adds more information, Panel C has a set up, Panel D is the hilarious punchline. Learning to use, or not use, panels effectively is a lifelong exercise, but one every cartoonist is dedicated to mastering. Eventually panel structure and layout will become as easy to you as writing sentences and paragraphs. It can be helpful to analyze your favorite cartoonist by *thumbnailing* a comic or two of theirs and see how they use panels.

Unlike thumbnails, which can be drawn on any old piece of paper or digital tablet, the actual comic you want to make should be on good paper. A good smooth bristol board paper is best for most beginning cartoonists. Bristol board holds ink well, is sturdy, and has been the gold standard for cartoonists stretching back a hundred years. There are different qualities out there, but most art stores will carry basic bristol board.

Invest in a drawing board. I don't mean a drafting table. Those can help when you are working on pages and pages of comics in the future. A drawing board is a light piece of wood or plastic you can put your paper on when cartooning. I've used a foam-core 14-by-19-inch drawing board for 10 years now. I use it more than my drafting table when working on comics. It is light, sturdy and portable. All the pros use them and they are usually no more than 30 bucks.

*Penciling.* Most cartoonists when starting out get lost in this step. What pencil do I use? Plain old No. 2? Do I use a mechanical pencil or a wooden one? What kind of eraser should I get? What about colored pencils, some cartoonists use them, right? My pencil lines are too dark! I'm ruining my paper with erasing too much! AUGH!!!!!!!

*Relax.*

You can do this.

Just remember this truth: *Pencils don't matter.*

I don't mean penciling isn't important. What I mean is, this part of the cartooning process is not as important as most people believe. They don't matter because the reader will never see them—unless you want to specialize in pencil-only comics.

Penciling tips that I wish I knew: when starting out, a mechanical pencil is the way to go. I recommend using a hard lead. Usually 3H or 4H are good pencil leads to use. The harder the lead (the H means harder, B means softer) the lighter the line left on the page. Perfect. Later you can move to colored lead, specifically "non-photo blue" lead which disappears when exposed to the light of a scanner (thus, no erasing needed). Buy a good eraser; if it costs more than a dollar you are in the right ballpark. You could get kneaded erasers if you want. They look like gray silly putty and they don't leave behind crumbs like other erasers.

When it comes to penciling, don't worry that they may look messy and incomplete. That's ok. Every cartoonist working today has messy pencils. Some look more finished than others, but messy is the key. Think of penciling as the first and second drafts of a piece of writing. The thumbnails were the rough draft. Give yourself plenty of grace when you're working on penciling. It takes time to get to a place where you feel happy with pencils. We have all been through it.

You can find many good books and online resources to help you get better at penciling. Most help you understand how everything complex can be broken down into basic shapes. It's worth your time and effort to find these resources. Christopher Hart's *Everything You Ever Wanted to Know About Cartooning But Were Afraid to Ask* (Watson-Guptill, 1994) is a great starting resource that has served me well for decades.

*Inking* is the final piece to the comics puzzle for the beginner. Inking is the practice of covering pencil lines with ink. It's the last step in making the principal art for most comics. The lines you want to keep become permanent. Inking is an art which will take practice to master. I won't lie, it isn't an easy step. It's the final draft of a paper before you turn it in. You can only use so much white out to correct problems before you need to redraw something completely. Like penciling, take a few deep breaths and remember, with each line you draw, you are getting better. Each panel finished is another step on the road to mastering cartooning.

If you have never inked before in your life, I recommend using artist pens that come in sets from art stores. These usually have three or four thicknesses: extra fine, fine, bold and maybe a brush-tipped pen. Micron and Faber Castell are perfect brands for beginners. When you are ready for more adventurous inking check out JetPens.com and get a set of Japanese Manga brush pens or mechanical pens. Japan has the most robust comics culture in the world and they have the best tools on the marketplace. I have been using a refillable Pentel Pocket Brush from Japan for seven years. It is my go-to inking tool. When you feel like you want to explore some more, you can get into the world of dip pens and explore different nibs and techniques.

Inking is about adding definition and clarity to your art. Sometimes it's about emotion (a broken or shaky line can add tons of complexity to a panel). Take your time to explore how other cartoonists ink and practice in a sketchbook. Nothing feels more rewarding than erasing all your pencils and have nothing left on the page but the crisp, black lines of your finished comic.

Beyond that, it's rinse and repeat. Keep making comics and exploring different techniques when it comes to the basics of cartooning. There is a lot to explore, from hand lettering to adding color and shading digitally. When you are ready, learn how to scan and make your comics into printed versions. You have a lot of fun learning ahead of you.

**Making (Small) Piles of Dough**

James Sturm, founder of the Center for Cartoon Studies, told me once that if a cartoonist worried too much about making money rather than making good comics, he or she would fail. I didn't listen to him all that well when he told me that. It was early in my career and I was more concerned with making a living as a cartoonist than about the craft of cartooning. It took me a few years in the freelancing world to learn how to value my craft first and then seek a marketplace for it. Don't make the same mistake I did and think first about the finances and then think about the comics.

Cartoonists have a lot of opportunities in the world today. You don't even need to go to college or grad school to "break in." School can help with connections and meeting peers, but it is not a requirement.

The Internet is probably the best and worst place for beginning cartoonists. The best because you can easily build a portfolio anyone in the world can see, and the worst because there are a lot of people who want to take advantage of cartoonists online.

The first thing you should do is create a blog and begin to post comics. It will get you into the habit of putting work out publically and have you thinking of an audience for the work you are creating. Where you go from there is up to you. The following are a few examples of how you can begin to get your work published and get paid for it, it isn't exhaustive, but it's a good beginning:

*Traditional Newspaper Syndicates.* If you have developed a great traditional comic strip idea, then research the syndicates and their submission guidelines. Just know that each syndicate gets thousands of submissions for new comics each year but only choose to develop one or two. The starting salary of a syndicated cartoonist is about $20,000 to $25,000 per year—and in comic strips, you create work for each day of the year.

*Comic Book Publishers.* Whether Marvel, DC or another publisher like my personal favorite, Valiant, all comic book companies need new comics talent and have guidelines for how new artists can submit work. Most comic book publishers break their creation process down so you can specialize in inking, writing, drawing, or even lettering and coloring. Some publishers, like Dark Horse and Image comics, accept and respect works by single creators, whereas the bigger publishers will own your ideas for themselves.

*Indie Comics.* This is a wide-open frontier of the comics world. You can get your foot in the door by self-publishing and *tabling* (selling your work at a table) at small press and comics conventions. Selling your own work will build a small following and eventually you can catch the eye of independent comics and graphic novel publishers who often table at the same conventions. Many of the best graphic novelists working today began their careers by self-publishing small zine (magazine) versions of their work. You can also start a self-promoted webcomic and sell printed versions at conventions. The indie market won't make you a steady paycheck to begin with, but you can find a community that will support you and champion your work.

*Webcomics.* You can go as deep into this field as you want. Some people have found amazing success with webcomics. A few of my peers have turned their webcomics into bestselling graphic novels or careers as storyboard artists. It's worth noting that most webcomics begin as works of love and personal vision. It can take time before they become financial successes, but it is possible.

*Applied Cartooning/Illustrating.* My work is mostly in this field. Comics have uses other than to entertain or uplift. Sometimes comics are used to teach and inform. Applied cartooning is using comics to help a company or organization communicate their ideas more clearly to their audience. While there is a deep history of applied cartooning, it has only recently become more widely accepted in American businesses. A great example of applied cartooning is Scott McCloud's webcomic for Google Chrome which was commissioned by Google when they were launching their new browser.[19] I have found that one of the best ways to make a living today as a cartoonist is to offer these skills to local companies, agencies, and publishers. I have done applied cartooning work for the State of New Hampshire, Dartmouth College and the National Science Foundation. All it takes are the cartooning skills and a little courage to seek out these projects.

These are only a few of the many paths you can go down in the world of cartooning. Follow your own path and you will do some amazing work.

---

19 http://www.scottmccloud.com/googlechrome/

It only takes a few panels in a sketchbook to be a cartoonist. It will take a lifetime to master the medium. I look forward to reading your work in the future!

As they used to say: "See you in the funny papers."

# The Panther-Pawed Need of a Writer to Read

*By Tracy Groot*

*Not smash and grab, but rather find and keep;*
*Go panther-pawed where all the mined truths sleep*
*To detonate the hidden seeds with stealth*
*So in your wake a weltering of wealth...*

—Ray Bradbury

Spock and I have something in common: We can mind-meld. I'm the only 100 percent human who can do it, but you have to be in arm's length. So, instead of a cerebral download of Ray Bradbury's poem on the Need of a Writer to Read," I'll fall back on words, and those, panther-pawed:

William Faulkner: "Read, read, read. Read everything—trash, classics, good and bad, and see how they do it. Just like a carpenter who works as an apprentice and studies the master. Read! You'll absorb it. Then write. If it's good, you'll find out. If it's not, throw it out the window."[20]

Stephen King: "If you don't have time to read, you don't have the time (or tools) to write. Simple as that."[21]

Miguel De Cervantes: "Finally, from so little sleeping and so much reading, his brain dried up and he went completely out of his mind."[22]

I fear many writers never have a chance to go completely out of their minds because they don't read enough. They absorb the how-to books or how-to blogs. They list all the "right" books you should read to be a good writer. But can they quote Shakespeare from *heart*? Can they tell you why they'd like to wring Robert Jordan's neck? Can they say how they felt when they came upon "It's a far, far better thing I do" after the far, far better

20 William Faulkner, from *Conversations with William Faulkner*. Edited by M. Thomas Inge. University Press of Mississippi, 1999.
21 Stephen King, from *On Writing; A Memoir of the Craft*. Pocket Books, 2000.
22 Miguel De Cervantes, from *Don Quixote*. Penguin Classics, 2003.

thing *they* did, reading *A Tale of Two Cities* instead of a slick blog post on great writing?

Don't mistake me. I like the recommended how-to stuff. It's how I found Ray Bradbury's poem. But if we do not go off on our merry own with shovels on shoulders to where the mined-truths sleep, we will never encounter treasures unquoted. We'll never find the things that need to make it to the light of *our* day.

I didn't find my favorite Shakespeare piece upon Googling Shakespeare quotes. I found it when I read *A Midsummer Night's Dream*:

*The poet's eye in a fine frenzy rolling, doth move from heaven to earth, from earth to heaven; and as imagination bodies forth the form of things unknown, the poet's pen turns them to shapes, and gives to airy nothing a local habitation and a name.*[23]

This jewel was all about writing. No blog post told me about the spectacular *need* to roll my eye in a fine frenzy. No how-to told me to fashion shapes from my pen once my imagination bodied forth findings. I found this on my own, and with a wild cry upon discovery, fell upon it like a greedy dwarf and dug it out with the loving care of a Dead Sea Scroll archaeologist. I held the mined truth up to the light of my day, then stuffed it in my sack and made a furtive getaway.

Another gem came from *All Hallow's Eve*, by Charles Williams:

*He knew the validity of his own work—yet he knew also that he might be wrong, as innumerable unfortunate bad painters had been. There was no way of being certain. But at least he believed that painting* could *be valid, could hold an experience related to the actuality of the world, and in itself valuable to mind and heart. He hoped this painting might be that; more, he could not say.*[24]

Charles showed me how I felt about my own writing.

When we read we make discoveries, and quite often, don't know we've found something. Here's the beauty: All of what we read goes fast to the keeping of a place Tolkien called his compost heap. There, nothing is lost. Every scrap to the lumpy pile, consigned to the keeping of catalyzing magic. There they sit, these scraps of ours, for weeks or years or decades.

Then lo...

...from this pile leaps something *new*, a plot rescue or character insight or POV choice all because we habitually rained down the goods with our

23 William Shakespeare, from *A Midsummer Night's Dream*. Signet Classic, 1998.

24 Charles Williams, from *All Hallows' Eve*. Faber and Faber Limited, 1947.

reading. It's too freaking *beautiful* that something I enjoy as deeply as reading would produce a by-product I can use.

Know what happens in a compost pile? Over time, leftover veggies and yard waste *work upon each other*, they break each other down to *create something new*. Guess what some finished compost is called? Black gold! Our black gold shows itself ready for use through blue-flamed leaps of inspiration. Then we seize a pen and turn to shapes that which has bodied forth because the other half of panther-pawed is this:

*We pay attention to that which leaps.*

A recent leap from my heap came when I was minding my own business, reading *North and South* by Elizabeth Gaskell.

Toward the end of the novel, Margaret Hale goes to the sea. She is in contemplation about the past, present and future and must make some big decisions. Day after day she goes to the sea where she sits unmoving and silent. At last, she makes a decision and rises.

At last! She makes a decision! She rises!

Do you tremble?!

A blue-flamed leap presented Margaret's *ocean* as a writer's body of *words*. Margaret sat at the sea day after day, this creation not of her own making. She came away better. We writers go to words. We come away not only better, but with power to make things better for others.

A while back I watched *The Guardian*, a film about the Coast Guard starring Kevin Costner. He is in a training room and on the wall is this: "To water you have been called to serve. To water you must go."

We need to read because to words we have been called to serve. Margaret went off to make things better for someone who sorely needed it. We sit near our word ocean long enough and we can make decisions and rise, restored and with faculties of restoration.

Which scraps did *North and South* mix with to produce the thinking it did? I don't know! It's a marvelous mystery. Clearly it mixed with the snatch I caught on the wall of the Coast Guard training facility. Maybe also with a broken-off scrap from *Dune*, or *Little House on the Prairie*, or *A Long Obedience in the Right Direction*. Maybe from a story I *had* to read in high school, or maybe one I *wanted* to read. Much as I hated Steinbeck's *The Red Pony* when I had to read it for school, bits crumbled down to my heap, same as when I willingly read his *East of Eden* many years later.

Read, people, read! Then write, write. Pay attention to those blue-flamed leaps of inspiration! A flame won't ignite a thing unless brought close to material. Seize your pen and see what conflagration may be by shaping that which bodied forth. If you don't, you'll never have a chance to burn anything down.

What, then, shall you read?

Happy news. Do the Faulkner thing—read anything.

Myself, I engage in two categories of reading: that which I make myself read, and that which I cannot help but read. Let's call them Mean Books and Nice Books.

Mean Books for me consist of titles like the following: *The Inferno,* by Dante. *War and Peace. The Iliad. The Aeneid.* Some Shakespeare. Some classics. Some new fiction. Basically, if you have to make yourself read it, it's Mean. Mean books are typically more challenging to read, and, for various reasons, generally yield great satisfaction upon completion. When I finished *Paradise Lost,* I felt as though a cavern inside had been knocked wider, increasing capacity. Capacity for what? I don't know. I just felt bigger.

I can't recall the reason I picked up *East of Eden,* some 20 years ago in my thirties. I was likely on a self-educating quest, figured I should read Steinbeck, and chose one with no ponies.

I was utterly unprepared for this shattering novel.

It's is now a hallowed fave, one of my top fives. I haven't *been able* to read it since, it scored so deeply. I hope to once more before I leave this earth. If not, once was a great privilege.

Another top five which started out Mean, owing to my great dislike for *Great Expectations,* was *A Tale of Two Cities.* It became Nice, and I've read it several times. To my great surprise, *Great Expectations* also became Nice when I read it for a classics book club. I look forward to reading it again with gladness. Dickens is now a favorite author.

(I hated *Great Expectations* because I read it before I was ready. Teachers have a hard job. How do they know when a kid is ready for a classic? I'm a big fan of the idea that there is a time to read certain books. Ninth grade wasn't my time. Then, I also read some Hemingway short stories, forced to it by curriculum; I hated those stories, and since then, I tried but haven't quite reconciled myself to Ernie. Give me Steinbeck any day.)

Mean Books I pick up by force of will alone based on universal recommendation or book club. They almost always do me good, and sometimes just because it's good to accomplish something difficult. (Anyone read *Winter's Tale* by Mark Helprin? *All the way through?* I still don't know what the darned book is about. But it was pretty.) I've tried several times to get over the wall with *Les Miserables* and fell back each time. Now it's on the docket for my classics book club, and I look forward to scaling the beast with grim relish. *The Brothers Karamazov?* Mean. *Vanity Fair?* Mean. *War and Peace?* Cruel. And I can't wait to read them all. Robert Service: "Each to his work, his wage at evening bell, the strength of striving."[25] Mean Books are work. They yield strength. By the way—that quote came panther-pawed.

I don't have much to say on Nice Books. We know what they are and read them most. Nice Books are simply grand old Guilty Pleasure, and by *guilty* I mean I could shirk duty and read 'em all the livelong day. *The Chronicles of Narnia*, for the eight hundredth time, does nicely here for me, as do the Harry Potter books or an effortless Louis L'Amour. (Not that all Nice books are effortless. Take *The Once and Future King*. Nice, but not effortless.)

Nice Books can denote favored genres. Mine are: fantasy, science fiction, speculative fiction (anyone read Jasper Fforde?), an occasional western or mystery or thriller or YA novel (Susan Cooper, anyone? Brandon Mull? Frances Hodgson Burnett? Ellen Raskin?).

Books of high literary quality can fall into either category. Wendell Berry? Mean. (I may incur wrath on that one.) Robin McKinley? Nice. Ray Bradbury? Both. I can't get myself to read *Dandelion Wine*, though because of *Zen in the Art of Writing* and *Fahrenheit 451*, it'll likely slide into Nice once read. Same for Flannery O'Connor. Her stuff looks like I'll take a beating, but a good one.

Charles Portis crafted another of my top five. No one told me to read *True Grit*. I came by it panther-pawed, fell into it, haven't returned. Michael Shaara wrote *The Killer Angels*, Michael Blake wrote *Dances With Wolves*. Read only these three for a year straight, multiple times, one after the other. Come time, you'll write.

I wonder with anticipation at authors unfamiliar who will make it to my favorite list, all because I go to where the mined truths sleep.

Here are two panther-pawed things you can do to read more:

*Schedule your reading*. I'm a list person. It's how I get things done. Six days a week, I put "Read" on my daily list. Sometimes I qualify it: "Read 15 minutes. Read two chapters. Read book club stuff." If I schedule reading, it becomes non-negotiable. (By the way, Sunday is a free-for-all and I read whatever and as much as I jolly well please.)

---

25 Robert Service, from *Acceptable Words: Prayers for the Writer*. Edited by Gary D. Schmidt and Elizabeth Stickney. Eerdmans, 2012.

*Join or start a book club.* I participate in three. One is a yearly book club with my local library called The 32nd Winter Reading Club. We read 32 books between October 1 and May 1. (32nd Street runs through my town.) Another is my classics book club. We read only classics, mostly YA and Victorian literature. Another is a recently started Mean Mountain Book Club. We put 25 titles in a random selection app, and guess what our first book is? The quintessential Mean Book of all time, *War and Peace*. We laughed. (We groaned first, then laughed.)

A last word:

Don't bother reading "well." Just read. I hope you take a swing at the prigs who tell you only to read "well." Read whatever *you* want, especially in your not-for-book-club reading time, and listen to Faulkner: read trash, too. By *trash*, I'm not talking about trashy *content*; I'm talking about that which is trashily *written* (in your opinion), because it's true: You *will* learn from crappy craftsmanship. I used to fear crappy craftsmanship (say that ten times real fast) because I didn't want to start writing that way. But I've discovered a point of magic for writers who read: we are protected from absorbing bad craftsmanship. I don't know how, and if anyone figures it out, let me know. But rest easy: you will not pick up bad writing. You'll just learn how to avoid it.

Look me in the eye: You want to write better? Then do your job and read, so you can do your job and write.

Talk about a magnificent win-win.

Difficult
Anything Russian
Moby Dick
Meditations - Rousseau
M. Bovary

Nice
Jane Eyre
Austin
Alcott
Bonhoeffer
John Adams
Wilberforce

# III

# PUBLISHING YOUR WORK

# Of Chicken Salad and Book Proposals

*By A.L. Rogers*

**Restless and Slinging Mayo**

In the spring of 2007 I was a restless cafeteria cook. Although I enjoyed my job, I was caught in a triangle of confusion: My college degree was in music. My work experience was in food service. My hopes and dreams were in the publishing industry. *Maybe someday I'll even write a book,* I mused while flipping burgers. I believed that about as much as I believed the frozen patties spread across the grill were 100 percent beef.

The thing is, I started to get pretty good at cooking. I became a manager and had fun with it. Maybe food service *was* my future. I would put artistic dreams like books and music behind me and get a "real" job, become a "real" cook.

So I applied for a cook's assistant position at an elite cultural organization in Grand Rapids, Michigan—and I got the job. The Frederik Meijer Gardens and Sculpture Park boasts sculptures by world-renowned artists, a 15,000-square foot walk-through greenhouse (you'd think you were in the tropics in the dead of a Michigan winter), and a concert venue that has hosted Wynton Marsalis, Garrison Keillor and other luminaries. It was in *this* kitchen that I would begin my illustrious career. No more burger flipping for me.

The first dish I was told to prepare was chicken salad for a few hundred people. At my previous job, I had prepared chicken salad more times than I could count—typically for 300 to 500 people per meal. "This will be easy," I said to myself. You just take a 30-quart commercial mixing bowl and add gallons and gallons of real mayonnaise (never Miracle Whip), diced celery, chunked chicken, and the one ingredient that brings it all together: sliced red grapes.

I placed a cutting board neatly in front of me, a sharpened knife, and two bowls on either side of the board. One was for the whole grapes, the other for the freshly sliced grapes. Gallons of unopened mayo were stacked nearby. Then I heard the lead chef addressing me.

"What are you doing?" His voice had the same annoyed quality of an older sibling who says, "Don't touch my stuff and get out of my room."

"Um," I stalled. I was holding the recipe in my hand. Was this a trick question? "I'm slicing the grapes for the chicken salad."

"Don't do that," he said, as if I'd suggested that we all get together after work and watch the leftovers freeze. "Just put them in whole."

"Put them in whole?" I was incredulous and it must have showed. "Don't people choke on them?" (These were large grapes, after all.) "Aren't you supposed to slice the grapes in a chicken salad?"

He looked at me sideways, his annoyance mounting. Then he said loud enough for everyone in the room to hear, "You think I got time for that shit?!"

He laughed derisively at my silence. "No. You ain't slicing the grapes. Just put them in whole." There was more laughter. This time a few of the other cook's assistants nervously chuckled. "Like we got time to slice grapes around here," he grumbled.

I learned a lesson that day that seems embarrassingly obvious to me now: *Everyone makes chicken salad differently*. And although I quit that job after only three days (grapes aside, that environment was soul-sucking—lots of bickering, lots of ego), I am glad for the experience. Some things *must* be done a certain way. Sammy Hagar told us there's only one way to rock, and Jesus said there's only one way to God. But most other things in life—from chicken salads to career planning—can be customized.

Book proposals fall into this second category. No matter what anyone may tell you, there is no single way to write one. Click-hungry writers' websites post headlines like "The Only Way to Write a Proposal that Sells!"—but that's a lie. The truth is that each book proposal will be a little bit different from any other. If written well, they will be tailored to the project, and perhaps even to the publisher.

### The Essential Elements of a Book Proposal *or* A Recipe for Chicken Salad

What follows are the things I consider to be basic pieces that every proposal should include. The order I've placed them in makes sense to me, but don't read it as dogma. Arrange the elements in whatever order makes the most sense for the book you are proposing, and the editor or agent who will be reviewing your work.

**A title and subtitle.** Place your best title and subtitle on the first page of the proposal. If you have other options, consider including them later on in the proposal. With nonfiction, I like the title to intrigue readers and the subtitle to explain the content (e.g. *Zen in the Art of Writing: Essays on Creativity* by Ray Bradbury, or *Eat, Pray, Love: One Woman's Search for Everything Across Italy, India and Indonesia* by Elizabeth Gilbert). Your goal with this approach is to make your work stand out and be clearly understood.

With fiction, especially if you are not an established author, I recommend studying the market you are publishing into and devising a title that fits (e.g. one-word titles were all the rage for a while with paranormal and post-apocalyptic teen fiction: *Divergent, Twilight, Cinder;* other young adult titles were wordy and character driven: *Harry Potter and the Chamber of Secrets, The Mysterious Benedict Society and the Perilous Journey, Charlie and the Chocolate Factory*).

Regardless of your genre, keep in mind that most of the time your publisher will have the last say on your title and subtitle. It's best to assume that whatever you put down will be changed.

**A synopsis paragraph.** This paragraph includes a few sentences that sum up the book. Try to answer the following two questions in four sentences, and you'll have a synopsis paragraph: *What does the book include? What will readers get out of this book?* In marketing terms you are describing the book's features (what it includes) and its benefits (what readers get from their time with it).

If Charles Dickens were to write a synopsis paragraph for *A Christmas Carol* today, it might read something like this:

*In the novella* A Christmas Carol, *readers will follow a wealthy British miser, Ebenezer Scrooge, on a ghostly Christmas Eve adventure through his past and future. Over the backdrop of grimy London circa 1850, through astute dialog and dynamic characters, Scrooge discovers that ignorance about the suffering poor and his raging greed have left his soul black and his life friendless.* A Christmas Carol *will introduce readers to memorable characters they are sure to quote long after they've finished the book, and they'll be challenged along with Scrooge to consider areas of ignorance and want in their lives.*

**A hook.** The hook is one or two sentences that sum up the unique or marketable qualities of the book. When writing your hook statement, focus on what sets your book apart from possible competitors and describe why those properties will make the book sell.

If the Brothers Grimm had written a hook sentence for their work, it might have said, *This book is the only collection of German folklore ever compiled and it is written in language accessible to elementary-age children.*

**A description of the target audience.** It's tempting to think that your book will be interesting to every reader, but the truth is that no single book appeals to everyone. (Don't believe me? Find the *New York Times* Best Sellers list online. Look at the top five titles. Are *all* of those appealing to you?) Publishers want to see a specific audience identified, preferably one they can reach and one that will actually be willing to pay for your book. So describe your audience's basic demographic details and list a few other bits of information that indicate who they are. Fictitious example: *The target audience for "Tweet Like a Boss" is 22–35 years old, media savvy, interested in books on leadership and striving to build a career.*

**A table of contents.** All that's required here is a numbered list of your chapter titles. If you plan to include an introduction, section headings, index, or anything else, indicate that as well. You are showing the book's shape in one quick snapshot.

**A detailed outline.** This outline can include the same information as the table of contents, but it also includes a short paragraph describing each chapter and major section. The detailed outline is intended to give the reviewer a sense of how you will develop your book's theme, how the hook shapes the content, and what your major points and illustrations will be.

**An "about the author" section.** Focus on information relevant to your authorship of the book. Answer this question: *Why am I the right person to write this book?* Include related publication history.

**Platform information.** A platform is your means of reaching an audience. It can include the events where you speak, the size of your social media following, the number of subscribers to your newsletter or blog, the number of self-published books you may have sold, the networks or affiliations you have which are relevant to the book's topic, notable people who may be willing to endorse your book, and any media connections you may have.

**Sample chapters.** I like to read at least two sample chapters with each book proposal. Some publishers and agents have specific numbers of words or chapters they want to see. You can find out how much a given publisher wants to read by reviewing their writing guidelines online. If they have none posted, I suggest providing two chapters.

Send chapters that get at the crux of your book's premise, and make sure they are written and edited carefully. Self-editing is fine, but having a trusted friend edit your proposal is better. I wouldn't often hire a freelance editor because of the cost, but it can be done if you believe your writing could use a professional touch. It's a judgment call. You don't want to put too much money into a proposal that might not go anywhere. In my opinion, a knowledgeable friend will probably be able to catch your mistakes well enough. One or two typos will not sink a book proposal.

### Things You Don't Need to Worry About

**Font size, margin size, and other formatting minutiae.** Writing a book proposal is not the same as writing a college term paper. Editors will not check to see if you used the Times New Roman 12-point font or if your margins are exactly a half inch. (If they do, they have too much time on their hands.) The default settings on Microsoft Word are perfectly appropriate for book proposals. It's okay to deviate from those settings, but remember that "less is more" when it comes to unique fonts and out-of-the-box formatting. Your goal is to produce an easy-to-read, professional looking document.

**A detailed marketing plan.** Platform information is all you need. If your publisher has a marketing team, they will write their own promotional plan. Offer to help them execute their plan and to do your own promotions too—but don't worry about including specifics in the proposal. Detailed marketing discussions most often occur later in the publishing process, after the book's release date has been assigned.

**A cover design.** Most publishers have staff to handle the creation of your book cover. Book covers are generated later in the publishing process and the design is usually controlled by the publisher. There's no reason to create a cover for your proposal. They are usually ignored, and if they're perceived as cheesy or amateurish, they may make your writing seem weaker too. (Call it "guilt by association.")

### Things to Avoid

**Sending a handwritten book proposal.** *Don't ever do this.*

**Overusing bold, italics, underlines, and more than two or three fonts.** Too much of this kind of text highlighting looks cheesy. It can also give the impression that your content is weak. The editor may wonder why you felt a need to dress up the proposal. Just stick to one or two fonts and use other effects sparingly.

**Padding your proposal in any way.** Resist the urge to exaggerate your platform numbers or your publication history. Just present yourself and your work honestly and with confidence. The truth will win the day.

**Sending the entire manuscript.** If your manuscript is finished, mention that somewhere in the proposal (many proposals include a little subheading called "manuscript status"), but don't send the whole thing. Most editors and agents won't take the time to read it—in fact, they may find it overwhelming to even skim a full manuscript. Just send one or two of your best chapters—they are more likely to be read. If the editor or agent likes your work, they will ask you for more. *Caveat:* Some fiction publishers *do* want to see the whole manuscript with a proposal. Some children's book publishers also wish to see the whole manuscript at the beginning. Visit publishers' web sites to learn their specific submission guidelines.

### Miscellaneous Tips

Include a title page with your contact information. If you find an agent they may change the title page to include his or her information. Agents go about this differently, so just follow their lead.

Number your pages.

In all things, strive for concision and clarity.

Read your proposal aloud before you send it in. You could be amazed at the errors you find. (Microsoft Word's spelling and grammar checkers don't catch everything. For example, Word won't highlight this, but you'll catch the error while reading aloud: *In 2009 I launched my website in 2009.*)

If possible, have a friend who is a professional of some kind read through your proposal and point out any spots that seem weak or unusual. This friend doesn't need to work in publishing, just intuitively understand what a professional document looks like.

**Make Yourself a Sandwich *or* Take and ~~Read~~ Eat**

Writers are often stressed out by book proposals. They feel like mortgage applications or college term papers. My encouragement to you is this: Don't worry about it. Everyone feels this anxiety. Even the most experienced authors, those writers with a paragraph full of book titles in their byline, will tell you that proposals annoy, frustrate, or stress them too. It's just part of the process.

It may help to remember that book proposals don't all have to be the same. This chapter is meant to explain the essential elements. Take this essay and get started, one section at a time. Don't be afraid to tweak and experiment. Save your work, and show it to your trusted friends and writers' group members. Make the proposal look and sound authentically like you. Then reward yourself and go make a sandwich.

For the record: I always slice the grapes in my chicken salad—and I usually add a touch of ground pepper.

# Agenting 101: The What, Why, When and Hows of Literary Representation

## By Timothy J. Beals

"I'm ready to learn, please help me." That is how each violin lesson began for my brown-eyed, raven-haired daughters, Marie and Carmen. As they faced their instructor in her paneled basement studio, each one with a violin and bow tucked neatly under one arm, they bowed their heads gently, doing what they were taught in the Suziki music program, a method that emphasized focus, discipline and humility. I sat nearby on a plaid, threadbare couch. Then the work began. Mrs. Weaver patiently showed the girls how to work the bow with staccato precision as they played "Mississippi Hot Dog," and she would explain how to move their small fingers up and down the strings to achieve a melodic "Go Tell Aunt Rhody."

Have you ever had a special teacher or coach or mentor? A guide who commands respect and has earned it? One who has done the hard work of mastering the material or the game or the principles and delights to share what they know? A teacher who introduces you to those they know—other musicians, athletes, and students—enthusiasts like you, and experts like them?

This is the ideal relationship between agent and writer: the agent to guide and the author to do her part. An agent is not always the expert; authors often know more about their subject matter, intended audience and competition. But an agent should know best what publishers are looking for, which houses are best to work with, and how to effectively present your material.

So what exactly is an agent? Who needs one and when? Why is a good agent so hard to find? If you're ready to learn, let's explore together the role of literary agents and their indispensable value to your writing life.

***What*** **Is a Literary Agent?**

A good agent is more like a coach or sherpa than a leader or manager. They are there to guide and encourage, not command and control. Your agent is your business partner, allowing you to focus on writing your best. An agent knows the market inside and out—including both large and small publishers. They are acquainted with many editors, publishers and other industry professionals and get along well with most of them.

Most importantly, they know what kinds of material those publishers appreciate and want to see, and they keep up with changes and developments in the industry—and the industry is constantly changing. That's why the agents at Credo maintain a spreadsheet of more than 200 editors at more than 50 publishers, updating it monthly to reflect who's who and what's what. We track the movement of editors from one house to another, how one publisher has decided to drop its fiction line, or when another has added a children's department.

The best agents are good advocates, salespeople and negotiators. They have extensive experience as an agent and have made many sales, ideally in the same field or genre as your own. The really good ones earn a living almost entirely from commissions, and they charge reasonable commissions (15 percent is the industry standard). They respond to your work, questions and phone calls promptly; they are always honest, straightforward, and cordial.

The right agents are willing to work with you if your material needs some editing or rewriting, and they can provide good suggestions for doing that work because they are avid readers and understand what other thoughtful readers expect. They have a good sense of what each of your projects is worth, who is most likely to be interested in it, and how much to ask for it. They get your work out to editors promptly and follow up on every submission, letting you know which editors have seen and are currently considering your material.

A good agent continues to present your work to editors even after it has received some rejections. They let you know promptly when they have stopped trying to sell a piece that has been repeatedly rejected, and immediately permits you to market or self-publish that piece on your own.

Once your project has been sold, their work continues as they read and negotiate contracts carefully, thoroughly and shrewdly. They also get you money, royalty statements and important information promptly, and forward any mail, inquiries and offers promptly.

Finally, the right agent will support you in your efforts to write what you wish to write, rather than what is popular this month, or what a publisher has most recently asked for. She believes in you and your ability as a communicator, encouraging you to write your best. She is a cheerleader, an advocate and your biggest fan. I had one unpublished but highly accomplished author come to me from another agency because her agent was reticent to promote the author's clear writing vision; instead the agent substituted her own idea about what was best for the author. After we began working together and focusing on her unique passion and message, the author's first book earned immediate interest from eight publishers, so we had the luxury of broad support and multiple offers. That book was the right book because it was the one my author was uniquely prepared to write and the one publishers were eager to champion.

**_When_ Do You Need a Literary Agent?**

Look for a literary agent when you are in the process of writing a book *and* have prepared a well-written book proposal that includes two or three sample chapters, not *after* the book has been completed. You serve your own interests best by taking this approach. If a publishing house is interested in the book you propose to write, the editor will likely want to work with you to shape the rest of the book, and that is made a lot easier if the manuscript is not already written.

If you already have a complete manuscript, however, don't offer that information to an agent or publisher unless you are asked. Instead, develop a great book proposal and present that. You can then edit or modify your manuscript as necessary to meet the agent or publisher's needs.

You will also want to seek out a literary agent when a publisher offers to buy a book that you have submitted on your own—to protect your interests and help work out the best deal possible. (A great agent can add up to 30 percent more value to the contract compared to negotiating a contract on your own.) Publishers will frequently recommend or require an agent before they agree to buy your manuscript.

**_How_ to Find a Literary Agent**

This can be the hardest part of the entire process, identifying the best agent for your work. But there is no short cut. Do your research, starting with these resources:

*Guide to Literary Agents*. A reference book; published annually. Contains a comprehensive list of agents. Provides limited information on each agent.

*Writers' Handbook*. A reference book; published annually. Includes a complete list of agents for the US market, plus separate entries for literary representatives in Canada, the UK and Ireland.

*Writer's Market*. A reference book; published annually. Includes a much shorter list of agents, but each agent's interests, specialties and credentials are described in excellent detail.

*Jeff Herman's Guide to Book Publishers, Editors and Literary Agents*. A reference book; published annually. Includes a comprehensive list of agents, including their interests, specialties and experience—over 300 pages long!

For an online list of top agents and agencies, visit the website of the Association of Authors' Representatives at http://www.aaronline.org/.

Specialized Lists of Agents:

*Children's Writer's and Illustrator's Market*. A reference book; published annually. Contains a list of many of the agents who handle material for children and young adults. Each listing is very thorough.

*Christian Writers Market Guide*. A reference book; published annually. Includes a chapter called "Literary Agents" with a list of agents and agencies representing Christian authors.

*Dramatists Sourcebook*. A reference book, now in its 26th edition. Includes many of the agents who handle material for the stage.

You should ask other people for information about agents they have worked with or know. Ask about agents' effectiveness, responsiveness, willingness to stick with a project, knowledge of the market, strengths and weaknesses. People you might talk to include:

Writers you know.

Editors and publishers with whom you have established a professional relationship (even if you've never sold them anything).

Members, officers and staff of any professional writers' organization to which you belong.

College professors of creative and professional writing. Many of these people have agents or knowledge of and experience with agents.

Faculty and organizers of writers' conferences and events.

### *How* to Approach a Literary Agent for Representation

After writing a book proposal that includes two or three sample chapters, make a list of agents that seem appropriate for you and your work using the resources listed above. Do *not* send unsolicited proposals or manuscripts to agents; send a query email first. A query is a message to an agent that describes a piece of writing and asks if the agent would like to see it (see "How to Query an Agent" below). Make your inquiry by email. No snail mail or blind phone calls. You may write to as many agents at a time as you like—eight to ten is typical—but send each email individually, *not* to a group list. That is the surest way to be ignored! Address the recipient by name.

Expect responses in one to six weeks. Be wary of agents who take longer than six weeks. If an agent does not respond to your query, which is common, move on. You can assume you are being deliberately ignored.

Send your book proposal only when requested by an agent. If several agents ask to see your work, email it to the one you like most, along with a brief note thanking the agent for their interest and reminding them of their request to see your manuscript. (If an agent requests your project while another agent is looking at it, say so straightforwardly and offer to show them the piece if you cannot work something out with the other agent.) If an agent turns down your query or proposal, merely thank the agent for his or her time and consideration and move on. Continue this process until an agent agrees to represent your project.

### *How* to Query an Agent

Here are seven tips for being professional, friendly, and effective when making that all-important first contact with an agent.

Write to an agent by name, or by name and title (for example, Marty Klein, Senior Agent), not merely by title or agency. "Dear Sir / Madame" is probably the most frequent mistake we see. If you haven't taken the time to get to know the agency and its personnel (including what they're actively seeking and what they're not representing), agents will assume you're just prospecting, not searching strategically. The facts you need should be prominently displayed on the agent's or agency's website, including clear submission guidelines and contact information. If they're not, be cautious.

Do not use Mr., Ms., Mrs., or Miss unless you are sure of the person's gender, marital status, and preference. Instead, write "Dear Marty Klein."

Make your query brief. It may be (and should be!) as short as two or three paragraphs. No more than one page if submitted as an attachment; no more than two page views if included in the body of your email.

Begin your query by introducing yourself. Include any *relevant* information about yourself, your credentials, your platform and your writing—any significant writing awards or fellowships you've received, any significant and clearly related advanced study in writing and your previous publications. List your previous relevant sales and publications; if you have several, stick with the major ones. In either case, only mention the ones likely to impress the agent.

In a separate paragraph, explain your project. Mention the title and a few words of description. If it is nonfiction, explain its theme, audience, approach, purpose, overall content and how it is distinctive from other books on the same topic. If it is fiction, write a very brief plot synopsis. Explain what makes your piece unusual or what special experience you have had that informs it.

Do *not* mention any of the following in a query:

Who has read and rejected the piece.

What anyone else has said about the piece (unless it is a well-known published author).

How long and hard you've worked on the piece.

Acknowledgment of others for their assistance.

Any admission that the proposal and samples are in less than ideal shape. (If they still need work, don't send queries to agents yet!)

A request for comments, criticism, advice or instruction.

How thrilled you would be to see your work in print.

Anything about your life not strictly relevant to your submission.

The rights you wish to sell.

How much money you want for the piece (or any discussion of price or payment).

End your message by asking if the agent would care to review the proposal, and thank him or her for the time and consideration.

### *How* to Work with an Agent

Once you've secured the services of an agent, continue making professional contacts, gathering information, seeking endorsements for your work and building your social media platform. Be polite, straightforward, honest and businesslike at all times. Sometimes the author-agent partnership turns into a real friendship, but it is first and always a business relationship.

Write or call your agent whenever you need to, but otherwise be patient and stay out of their inbox and voicemail. Instead, your agent will write or call whenever there is news to report. If you have heard little or nothing from your agent, however, it is reasonable to call or write every two months to see what has happened.

After you have agreed to let an agent represent your next project, provide the following information:

The names of any editors or publishers who have asked to see your work.

The names of any editors or publishers who have read and enjoyed your earlier work.

The names of any editors or publishers you do *not* want your work submitted to.

The names of any editors or publishers who have already seen and rejected your project in its current (or very similar) form.

Whether part or all of the project has been previously published, and if so, where, when and by whom.

Don't expect your agent to make decisions for you. Agents will bring you offers, answer your questions and make suggestions, but only you can decide what to accept, what to turn down or when to ask for more. Indeed, this is part of your responsibility as an agented author. If your agent does not automatically send you a list of the people and organizations to which your project has been submitted, feel free to request it. Then allow your agent a reasonable amount of time to sell your work. Two to six months is typical.

If you ever have a problem with your agent, write or call them to discuss the issue. Be honest, firm, direct and calm. Remember that your agent has many other clients. Expect them to be responsive and helpful—but don't expect constant and immediate availability.

Don't let publishers make an end run around your agent. If you are approached directly about a project your agent is representing, get the person's name, email address and employer, and pass on this information to your agent, who will take things from there. This is not only good business, it's your legal obligation. It doesn't happen often that publishers bypass an agent, and it's usually unintentional. But unless you are working directly with an editor on your manuscript, refer all inquiries to your agent for resolution or negotiation. You'll be glad you did.

If you want to discuss an idea for a new project, or if you require some professional advice, feel free to call or email your agent. Ask him whether or not he would be interested in seeing your next project. He may decline to represent future projects you propose, but if you've been successful in the past, he should welcome new ideas. Simply send each new project to your agent with a brief message, and expect a prompt response.

So are you ready for an agent? Do you want to make beautiful music together? Come prepared, practice your craft, stay humble and play your part. The right agent can guide your writing, present your work to the right editors and effectively manage the business side of publishing on your behalf. Many publishers require writers to have an agent, and most successful writers work with one. So be ready to learn and your agent will help with the rest.

# Keep Your Editor(s) on Your Side

*By Paul Kent*

Let's imagine that all your hard work has paid off: You've earned a contract for a book. Congratulations! Go ahead and order that big slice of cheesecake. This is worth celebrating.

And it's worth duplicating, if at all possible.

Future deals depend on many factors, including your level of sales success. While that's not entirely in your hands, here's advice for something that is—keeping your editors on your side.

That thrilling document entitled "Publishing Agreement" indicates you've already won over your acquisitions editor. Depending on the size and structure of the publishing house, you may work with other editors at the substantive (or developmental), line and copy-editing levels. Or perhaps those various levels will be combined in some way and handled by one or more editors. Whatever the case, do all you can to develop a good working relationship with her, him, or them—it won't guarantee you another contract, but it sure can't hurt. And, honestly, it's just the right thing to do.

For the purpose of this essay, we'll assume that you have an engaging story to tell and that you're a talented writer. Rather than parsing grammar and punctuation rules here, let's consider ways to make the editing process—of *your* book!—run smoothly. Let's discuss a few procedural matters, as well as some relational insights, that will help to keep your editors on your side.

As an in-house editor for many years, I have loved those authors who mind their proverbial p's and q's—they turn in clean, strong manuscripts that have obviously been through multiple drafts; they verify details and provide all necessary sourcing; they respect my time, insight and experience in the industry. Their text isn't necessarily perfect (otherwise, they wouldn't need me at all), but they've demonstrated expertise and professionalism in the writing process. Then, during the editing, they seriously consider my recommendations for improvement.

The writers who don't do these things? Well, let's just say editors aren't quite as eager to work again with them. Here's an example, which I admit is extreme—but also 100 percent true: a freelance writer once introduced himself by email, offering his services in particular genres, then followed up over the next few years until what I thought was an appropriate project arose. We agreed on terms and executed a contract, and he got to writing . . . I guess. In the end, he bailed out of my project, while muffing another manuscript he was writing for one of my coworkers. That project was a month overdue (beyond a revised deadline), incomplete ("as done as it's going to be," he said), and just not good (which he readily admitted). Would I and my fellow editor ever consider working with this guy again? Are you familiar with the phrase, "Not in a million years?"

Under normal circumstances, every one of us—author and editor alike—aims at the same target: a compelling book that meets some need in the marketplace. (Ideally, in meeting that need both author and publisher make money, which is certainly an additional impetus to succeed.) As with any human endeavor, though, "little things" can create frictions that interfere with our overall goals. But I hope this insider's perspective will go a long way toward keeping your publishing road smooth and clear.

So, whether you're an up-and-coming writer or you've been around the block a few times, here are Ten Big Ideas for keeping your editors on your side:

**Rewrite, rewrite, rewrite.** Apart from the stone tablets that Moses brought down from Mount Sinai, *every* manuscript can benefit from a rewrite. Actually, several rewrites. Yes, they take time and energy, and there's every possibility that you'll be on a tight (we might even say "crazy") schedule—but rewrite anyway. Now that you've earned that contract, you're a professional, so put forth the extra effort that designation demands.

Let me make a practical suggestion: read your manuscript aloud, and listen for clutter—things like really, very, extremely unnecessary adverbs and adjectives; sentences which have been written in a passive voice; the utilization of sesquipedalian verbiage—then clean it up. Afterward, you'll have dealt with unnecessary adverbs and adjectives, passive-voice sentences, and the use of long terms . . . and tightened your manuscript by nine words. (You realize what I was doing there, right?)

Sure, it's your editors' job to back you up on this, but why not give them a head start? Trust me, they'll notice and appreciate it.

**Root out plagiarism.** "What? I would never plagiarize!" Not consciously, I'm sure, but I've happened across enough examples in my editing career to make it worth running up a red flag. I believe most instances of plagiarism are innocent—simple oversights rather than intentional cheating. But they certainly look bad. If during my fact-checking I find a word-for-word (or only slightly revised) passage from another book or from a web site like Wikipedia, I get nervous.

As you reread and rewrite your manuscript (see #1), pay special attention to the examples and explanations you've drawn from other sources. If you have any at all, make sure you've completely rewritten that information to make it your own, or that you've credited the original source. Or maybe both.

The fact that your manuscript is completely free of plagiarism may not register with your editors. But be sure that they'll react to a trouble spot. Your special care here is like buying insurance for your home or car—it's not necessarily fun, and it comes at a cost—but it prevents a lot of headaches down the road.

**Quote with caution.** You know what Abraham Lincoln said: "The problem with quotes on the Internet is that you can't always be sure of their authenticity." I'd like to shake hands with the genius who started that little meme, and whoever extended the irony by inserting an image of Benjamin Franklin or George Washington over Lincoln's name . . . it's a brilliant way of illustrating the dangers of online quotes. Don't trust every inspirational image you see on Facebook, LinkedIn or Twitter, and be wary of those Web sites on which the users post quotes . . . in my own editing, I have often found them to be misattributed.

You'll impress your editors by double-checking the quotes you want to use via Amazon's "Look Inside" feature, through Google Books, or even on a web site like QuoteInvestigator.com—its carefully sourced explanations give me a lot more confidence than this attribution I once saw on a quote site: "My sixth-grade classroom wall."

Ideally, you should quote from books you've read yourself, ones for which you understand the context and know the author of the material. Even if you find an accurately worded quote that seems like a perfect fit for your manuscript, do you want to find out later that the author is a white supremacist or a convicted child abuser?

**Use with permission.** Generally, brief quotations from other books fall under the legal doctrine of "fair use"—there is no need to request permission from a publisher if you reproduce the words accurately and give them appropriate credit. The doctrine is a bit vague—no law or court has ever produced a specific formula for determining what "use" is "fair"—so most publishers have their own rules of thumb, often a word count threshold like 75 or 100 from any particular source. If you plan to use longer excerpts, your publisher will probably expect *you* to pursue an official permission, most likely with a form your editor will provide. Be advised that this process can take a while, so if you have to do it, don't procrastinate.

The idea of "brief quotations" does *not* apply to poetry or song lyrics. These copyright holders are very protective of their material and almost always demand written permission (and a fee) to use even a line or two. It stands to reason: if "fair use" is based on the percentage of material drawn from an entire work, two lines from a 16-line song is a much larger use than a hundred words from a 300-page book.

A final thought about using other writers' words: While it's a common and honorable way to bolster your own arguments or provide some point of interest to your readers, be careful not to rely too heavily on quotations. Always remember that this is *your* book—be confident, and show your editors and readers that you're the expert.

**Give me sources (or give me death).** Not every book needs notes, but if yours does, take care of them early—otherwise, they can burn a lot of valuable time and energy during the editing process. I suggest that, as you write your manuscript, you fully footnote every quotation in accordance with guidelines in *The Chicago Manual of Style*. And, while you're at it, why not produce a complete bibliography as well? It will be easier for the publisher to remove these things if they're ultimately not needed than for you to try to assemble them (under duress) during the editing process.

Of course, compared to your writing, things like notes and bibliographies are much less important—readers want a compelling experience with your text, not your back matter. But if you or your editor believe you need these elements in your book, do everyone a favor by handling them with care, sooner rather than later.

**Talk to me!** Feel free to ask your editor questions. There's no harm or embarrassment in clarifying matters like sources, permissions and quotations, or other things such as schedules, technical issues regarding your files, even writing and editing philosophies. Authors and editors are a team, and we'll work best together when we're on the same page. (Please note that occasional publishing-oriented clichés are always appropriate.)

Early in the process, your editors will likely introduce themselves, explaining many of these matters and how they specifically relate to your manuscript. Consider their comments carefully, and ask them to elaborate when necessary—whether to clarify a point they've made or to address an issue they've overlooked. It's far better to ask a "dumb question" than to make a wrong assumption—because wrong assumptions usually create more work for your editors and yourself.

**. . . But please respect my time.** The flipside of "talk to me" is "don't monopolize the conversation." While your book is probably the single biggest thought in your mind, your editors are dealing with numerous other projects at the same time. Yes, they're excited to be part of your book, but no, they don't have exactly the same focus you do.

Early on, find out how your editors prefer to communicate. I would much rather use email than talk on the phone, but I once worked with an author who was my exact opposite—and will never forget the two-hour, 22-minute phone call we had to discuss proofreading corrections. I think it left a permanent kink in my neck.

In that case, I was dealing with a more established and successful author, so the scaled tipped a bit more his way. That's not to say that a less experienced author should expect disrespect from his or her editor—but it does illustrate the fact that the vast majority of us will have to earn our privileges. Once we've paid our dues and shown we can do a job, we enjoy more freedoms—even in the editing of our manuscripts.

Just a couple of practical suggestions here: first, "collect your thoughts" before communicating with your editor. By that I mean don't shoot off quick emails with whatever individual questions or concerns enter your mind—jot each one down, think it over, and if the issue doesn't ultimately resolve itself, send it with a few other matters in a single message. But try to avoid the opposite danger, too. Don't wait too long to ask your questions, sending a whole list in one mammoth, overwhelming email. You always gain points by being respectful of your editors' time.

**Speaking of time—be punctual.** This is huge, since the publishing process is very susceptible to the domino effect. In the pursuit of a successful release of your book, you're part of a team that includes your publishing company editors, designers, marketers and production department, as well as out-of-house players such as booksellers, promoters and even reviewers. That's a lot of moving parts, and a glitch anywhere in the system can pose real problems. One delay can lead to another, jeopardizing the release plans—and your ultimate success.

Of course, hiccups just happen sometimes and publishing teams do their best to adapt and keep books moving along. Your job as an author is to do everything you can to meet the dates your editors give you—your initial manuscript deadline, of course, and then those target dates for revisions, editing reviews, proofreading checks, whatever. When you're punctual, your editors' job is easier and they'll appreciate your effort. (And you'll be doing your own book a favor.)

**Be yourself.** If this essay, written by a long-time, full-time editor, has in any way implied negativity toward authors, please understand that that was not my intention. I want to help you understand the editorial process, and to know what's helpful and unhelpful, appreciated and not appreciated by editors. But I will be the first person to applaud you as an author for what you do. You have done the heavy lifting—coming up with an idea, devoting the hours of research and writing and revision that manuscripts demand, putting yourself out before the public and risking possible rejection—but also enjoying the exciting possibility of popularity and financial gain. You've accomplished something that the vast majority of other people only think about—so pat yourself on the back and say, "Yeah, good for me."

So be yourself, all through the process. As you write, trust your instincts—project your own voice and don't try to be anyone but yourself. During the editing process, seriously consider the suggestions your editor makes but be ready to stand your ground when necessary. If your editor has missed the point (it *can* happen), respectfully explain why your way is correct. Give-and-take is to be expected, since the ultimate goal is the best possible experience for your readers. Just always remember that your editor is a reader too—one of your very first.

And so we arrive at the last of our Ten Big Ideas for keeping your editor on your side:

**Send cheesecake.** Not really. Okay, maybe. Well, seriously—just treat your editors the way you'd like to be treated. That "Golden Rule" applies to every area of life, even the wild-and-woolly world of publishing.

Congratulations on your book contract—either the one you have already gotten or the one your hard work and persistence will lead to. You've done well to reach this point, so keep the ball rolling and finish strong. I wish you much success and some tremendous personal fulfillment!

# Bookstores Are an Author's Best Friend

*By Josh Mosey*

Writers write books. Bookstores sell books. Pretty straightforward. Except that it isn't.

The relationship between writers and bookstores is both complementary and complex.

As we explore this relationship, it could be helpful to define what I mean by "bookstores." Technically speaking, any establishment that sells a book could be called a bookstore. The bookstores that I refer to are specifically independent bookstores. By that, I mean brick-and-mortar establishments that are staffed by professionals who decide which books appear on the bookshelves. The trouble with bookstore chains—even if they carry the same inventory—is that their employees are not required to be as knowledgeable about industry trends. Most chains experience a higher employee turnover rate which would make long-term relationships difficult to foster.

That isn't to say that chain bookstores or even big box stores like Costco and Sam's Club aren't great places to buy books. I'm just saying that it will be more difficult for employees of those stores to hand-sell your book or help with promotional events.

Think for a minute about your favorite bookstore. Yes, they have all the books that you want. But they also carry the books that you didn't know you wanted. And the books are only the first and most obvious part of a great bookstore. The greatest bookstores are set apart by their staff.

Bookstore employees love books. They are intimately involved in selecting books that their customers will love. They can read marketplace trends as easily as they read the books themselves.

There are benefits to having a strong relationship with an independent bookstore.

**Case Study: Susie Finkbeiner**

Susie Finkbeiner is an author of contemporary and historical fiction. Her publishing career began with the book, *Paint Chips*, from a small publishing house. Today, she's fulfilling a multi-book contract with a larger publisher. Susie also happens to be a loyal friend to her local bookstore.

"I've talked with Chris more than a few times to get ideas for comp titles as well as to make sure that a plot idea I had was fresh and not overdone. I've also talked to Darron about how certain genres perform compared to others."

In a recent online promotion from the bookstore, one of Susie's books faced off against books from highly prolific authors like Beth Moore and Beverly Lewis. For the promotion, books were placed in a March Madness-style bracket and voted on. The winner of the competition would be placed on sale and given a prominent display in the store. Susie's book won hands down and continues to be a great seller for the bookstore!

**Bookstores Can Help You During the Writing Process**

As Susie pointed out, if you are looking for direction for your novel, bookstore employees can tell you which plot devices are overused. They know what type of characters are populating the bestsellers. They can point you toward trending topics or gaps in the marketplace. No, they won't write the book for you, but they can help you avoid some of the stumbling blocks that prevent books from being written.

Don't overlook the possibility of using the bookstore as a place to write your book. A lot of bookstores double as coffee shops and you'll be surrounded by the evidence that your dreams of writing are achievable.

**Bookstores Can Help Get Your Book Published**

One of the keys to a well-written book proposal is an accurate list of comparable titles. By placing your book next to other books already on the market, the list gives acquisition editors a frame of reference to understand the type of book you hope to publish. It helps a publisher's marketing team understand the audience you are aiming for. And it gives salespeople the tools to help other booksellers place the books within their stores. If you want an in-depth understanding of which books to compare to yours, a bookstore employee who understands your work can point you toward the most fitting options, rather than simply the biggest names from your specific genre. (Pro tip: If you compare your book to a list of international bestsellers, no one in publishing will believe you or give you the time of day.)

**Bookstores Can Help Sell Your Book**

One of the best sales tools that authors have is an advocate in a bookstore who facilitates word-of-mouth advertising. Longtime readers itching for new titles trust the opinions of bookseller friends. If your book is on their lips, it won't be long until it is also in the shopper's baskets. And when it is time for your book's release, publishers love being able to throw book release parties in venues where book sales are reported to the *New York Times* bestseller lists.

**Case Study: Sharon Garlough Brown**

Baker Book House in Grand Rapids, Michigan is one of the top independent bookstores within the Christian Booksellers Association. Founded in 1939 by Herman Baker, it began as a used book shop, stocked with Herman's own books. Today, it is still known for its used books, but it is also known for its wide selection of fiction books, theological texts, children's books and greeting cards, and its gift department. The store manager also happens to be the chairperson of the CBA and contributes regularly to publishing trade magazines. When Baker Book House does something new, publishers and other indie bookstores take notice.

One question that publishing sales representatives often ask of Chris Jager, Baker Book House's fiction buyer, is, "What is your number-one bestseller in Fiction?" Chris's answer never fails to surprise these folks.

"Sharon Garlough Brown," responds Chris.

"Really?" is usually the salesperson's reply.

Now, let's take a look at why this is a surprising answer. There are many authors within the CBA who are better known: Karen Kingsbury, Ted Dekker and Beverly Lewis, to name a few. Each of those authors has dozens of titles to their name and they are published by some of the largest publishing houses in the Christian marketplace. Sharon Garlough Brown has only a few books so far, and hers are from a publisher who is better known for Bible study materials and academic books.

So what makes Sharon Garlough Brown the bestselling fiction author at a place like Baker Book House?

Long before she was a published author, Brown was a loyal shopper. She developed relationships with the store's manager and employees. And she keeps those relationships with frequent visits and conversations.

She's also an avid self-promoter. With each new release, she has been willing to host a book launch party at the store, inviting all of her friends and family to come out and celebrate with her. Beyond that, she uses the social networks where she is present to let people know that Baker carries her book and that her fans should buy it there.

Baker Book House is happy to have many relationships like they enjoy with Sharon Garlough Brown, because it means that they'll sell more books and hold more events that bring shoppers into the store. And Brown is happy to have Baker Book House, because she knows that the employees there are hand-selling her titles, stemming from a personal relationship with the author.

But how do you go from being an unknown writer to a bookstore's best friend? There are five things to keep in mind when pursuing a strong relationship with a great bookstore.

**1. Research**

Learn everything you can about the store before making contact. How do they advertise themselves? Do they have experience running store events? Do they have strange hours? What is their customer base? You can usually find these things within a few clicks around the store's website and social media accounts. (If this were a relationship between two people instead of an author and a bookstore, this might be considered stalking.) Perhaps you will find out that approaching the store would be more hassle than your time is worth. If they are going to be a worthwhile contact, they will be impressed that you know who they are and what is important to them.

**2. First Contact**

Find out who will be your main contact at the store. If the bookstore is smaller, the main contact is probably going to be the manager. Many managers function as both buyers for their store as well as events coordinators. At larger stores, though, this may not be true. Where I work, at the aforementioned Baker Book House, different employees are responsible for buying fiction books, coordinating events, and marketing books and events within the store. If you want your book on their shelves, you'll need to talk to the buyer. Once the book is there, you may need to talk to the events person about organizing a book signing or in-store speaking engagement. Maybe you have a few ideas about marketing the book in a fresh way. In any case, it will be helpful for you to speak to the correct person.

**3. Communicate**

Once you have the right person, you need to have the right thing to say. Prepare your elevator pitch. If you don't know what that is, picture yourself on an elevator with the only person who can make your dream of publishing a reality. You only have a few seconds to convince them to publish your books. What do you say?

Your pitch should be short enough to convey your meaning quickly, but in-depth enough to keep them thinking about it. If your book has thematic similarities to familiar works, feel free to us them. For example, you could describe the Hunger Games books as Survivor meets Mad Max, but with teens.

Use this pitch when talking to bookstores who don't carry your book. Give them a reason to invite you in.

**4. Timing**

There is a reason that they didn't name it the "waiting for a cab" pitch or the "on the phone with important investors" pitch. Even if you have the best pitch in the world, if you choose the wrong time to deliver it, you'll do yourself more harm than good. For example, no one likes to be interrupted during lunch or when they are in the middle of a time-sensitive meeting. When talking to a bookstore, always try to set up a good time for your contact to speak. You want them to be attentive to your message.

**5. Follow-up**

After your first contact, follow up with a thank you, regardless of the turnout. Thank-you's are a class act and bookstore staffers always appreciate receiving them. If you want to set the tone for the rest of your relationship, a thank-you note or email will leave a positive impression with a bookseller. They are more likely to have your book on their lips next time a customer asks them for a recommendation.

If you've followed the steps above, I have no doubt that you understand the importance of bookstore relationships and that you are on your way to a fruitful relationship with one. Now let's walk through what happens when your book is ready to release from a publisher.

The amount of marketing support varies from publisher to publisher and from book to book. Let us assume that in order for your book to be successful, you'll handle a lot of the marketing yourself. The good news is that publishers love self-promoters, even when they spend money on marketing your book.

Just like you did when you crafted your book proposal, you need to understand your book and your audience. After it has been edited and revised a few times, your book may no longer look like the proposal, so it may be a good idea to jot down a fresh synopsis and comparable title list. Just like publishers, bookstores can use these tools to target your book's promotion to the right customers.

Bookstores love when authors visit, because it gives them a fresh chance to get people in their doors. They will be counting on you to spread the word in your community circles, just as they will be spreading the word in theirs.

Most bookstores have the ability to delve into their customer database and pull physical and email addresses for customers who have purchased similar titles to yours. If nothing else, if the store is engaged in social media, they will be able to target their own fans as well as those by similar authors.

If you really want to wow a bookstore, come prepared with marketing materials and a plan. Here are a few suggestions for useful promotional items:

Bookmarks
Postcards
Flyers
Posters
E-Blasts
Social Media Images (sometimes called "shareable graphics")

If a bookstore has its own marketing team, they may be able to take the images that you supply and integrate them into their store's branded materials. If it is a smaller bookstore, they will appreciate whatever you have that they won't have to make for themselves.

Another useful tool for bookstores is a timeline. Marketing plans often start with a sales projection and then work backward from the time of release. If your book has not yet been released, here's a rough plan to follow when promoting your book release or launch event.

ASAP—list the event on the store website, send event info to local media

One month to event—hang posters, send postcards

Two weeks to event—send e-blast, put flyers in customer bags at cash register

One week to event—cashiers and other bookstore staff mention the event to customers

Days prior to event—reminder e-blast, social media posts (this is a great time to use the shareable graphics you made)

As a reminder, make sure that you are familiar with a store before contacting them. Ideally, you'll be working with more bookstores than just the one that you know best. Look up their website, their events list, etc. If possible, visit the store in person. The more you know about the bookstore, the better you are going to look in their eyes.

Arrange a meeting by phone or in-person with the store manager, relevant book buyer, or events coordinator to discuss your book event and the marketing of it. Keep timing in mind when choosing a date.

(Pro tip: Be sure to make sure that your event date does not conflict with something of interest to your audience. Our bookstore staff learned this the hard way one year when, months in advance, we schedule a major event with a bestselling author that happened to fall on the same day as a Detroit Tigers World Series game. Our store is in Michigan and we evidently serve lots of baseball fans because our attendance was really poor that night. Though we couldn't have predicted a World Series game when we scheduled the event, the lesson was still a valuable one: pay attention to the events and interests of your audience before scheduling an event.)

Finally, ask if you can send the bookstore a timeline. Once the date for the event is set, promote the event yourself.

Everything you do with the store reflects back on you. By delivering on your promises, and providing a store with helpful materials, you create trust with the store and a reason for them to hand-sell your book.

After the event, and regardless of whether people showed up or not, send a thank-you card to the store for the opportunity. Even if people didn't show up for the event, the card will reinforce your image and help retailers to sell your books by giving them a pleasant talking-point with customers.

No matter how much we wish that writing could work like it did in the olden days, before today's era when authors spend as much time and effort in promoting a title as they did when writing it, those days are gone. But you are not alone. Bookstores depend on authors to write the books that they will sell. They want you to succeed and they want to be part of your success.

So go find an independent bookstore today and introduce yourself. It doesn't matter where you are in the writing process. You could be a brand new writer with nothing published, or a veteran with numerous publications to your name. If you support a bookstore, they will support you.

# About the Contributors

**Zachary Bartels** is the author of several critically-acclaimed suspense novels. His debut, *Playing Saint,* has been called an "intrigue-filled thriller" (*Library Journal*) and "an exciting step forward for thrillers" (bestselling author, Cliff Graham) and was a finalist for the 2015 Inspy and Carol Awards. His follow-up, *The Last Con* (HarperCollins Christian Fiction) "will leave readers stunned" (*RT Book Reviews*). Zachary serves as pastor of Judson Baptist Church in Lansing, Michigan, where he lives with his wife Erin and their son. He enjoys film, fine cigars, stimulating conversation, gourmet coffee, reading, writing, cycling and co-hosting the popular "Gut Check Podcast." You can find more information about Zachary (as well as follow his blog, Twitter, and Facebook) at zacharybartels.com.

**Timothy J. Beals** has been president of the Credo Communications literary agency since 2005. He has also been an adjunct professor of publishing, editing and professional writing at Cornerstone University since 1989. Tim began his publishing career as an editor at HarperCollins Christian Publishing in Grand Rapids, Michigan. After 25 years of working for publishers large and small, Tim started his own agency in the service of authors and readers during a period of rapid change in the publishing industry. To learn more, visit credocommunications.net.

**Samuel Carbaugh** is an author, illustrator and cartoonist living in western Michigan. Sam is a graduate of the Center for Cartoon Studies and has worked for such wonderful folks as Dartmouth College, Nomad Press, Middlebury College, The State of New Hampshire and The Montshire Museum of Science. He has illustrated numerous books and in 2014 released his first book as both author and illustrator: *Comics: Investigate the History and Technology of American Cartooning* (Nomad Press). See samples of his work at samcarbaugh.com.

**Jeff Chapman** writes software by day and speculative fiction when he should be sleeping. His work ranges from fairy tales to fantasy to horror and ghost stories. Jeff's short stories have appeared in numerous anthologies and online publications. His novels include *The Black Blade: A Huckster Novel* and the forthcoming *The Breath of the Sea: A Westerlands Novel*. He lives with his wife, children and cats in a house with more books than bookshelf space. You can find him musing about words and fiction at jeffchapmanbooks.com.

**Robert G. Evenhouse** is a speaker, fiction writer and blogger living in Grand Rapids, Michigan. He is married, has four children and is always looking for that spare scrap of time to squeeze in a sentence or two. Robert is also a founding member of the Weaklings writers group that created the Jot Writers' Conference. Connect with him at robertevenhouse.com or on Twitter at @parttimenovel.

**Susie Finkbeiner** is bestselling author of *A Cup of Dust: A Novel of the Dust Bowl* and *A Trail of Crumbs: A Novel of the Great Depression*. She is a wife, mother, and story addict. Learn more about Susie and her work at susiefinkbeiner.com.

**S. D. Grimm's** first love in writing is young adult fantasy and science fiction. She is represented by Julie Gwinn of the Seymour Agency and author of *Scarlet Moon*. She currently has four books under contract, including the remainder of her YA fantasy series Children of the Blood Moon. When she's not writing or editing, Sarah enjoys reading (of course!), practicing kickboxing and Brazilian jiu jitsu, training dogs and binge-watching shows with great characters. Her office is anywhere she can curl up with her laptop and at least one large-sized dog. You can learn more about her upcoming novels at sdgrimm.com

**Tracy Groot** is the Christy Award–winning author of several historical novels with settings ranging from ancient biblical times to the American Civil War and WWII, including *The Brother's Keeper*, *Madman*, *Flame of Resistance*, *The Sentinels of Andersonville*, and *The Maggie Bright*. Tracy's novels have received starred Booklist and Publishers Weekly reviews and have been called "beautifully written" and "page-turning" by Publishers Weekly and "gripping" with "exquisitely drawn" characters by Library Journal. Tracy and her husband have three sons and a daughter-in-law and live near Grand Rapids, Michigan. Learn more at tracygroot.com.

**Alison Hodgson** is the author of *The Pug List: A Ridiculous Dog, a Family Who Lost Everything, and How They All Found Their Way Home.* She is a Moth StorySLAM winner and a regular contributor to the design website Houzz.com. Her writing has been featured in Woman's Day magazine, on Forbes.com, Christianity Today's Women, and the Religion News Service, and her essays have been published in a variety of anthologies. Alison lives in Michigan with her husband, their children and three good dogs. Connect with Alison at alisonhodgson.net, on Facebook @alisonhodgsonauthor, on Twitter @HodgsonAlison or on Instagram @therealpugoliver.

**Kenneth Kraegel** is the author and illustrator of *King Arthur's Very Great Grandson* (which was a *New York Times* Notable Children's Book of 2012) *The Song of Delphine,* and *Green Pants,* all from Candlewick Press. He is a self-taught artist who works primarily with pen and watercolor or pencil and watercolor. Visit him at kennethkraegel.com.

**Matthew Landrum** is associate editor of *Structo Magazine.* His poems and translations have recently appeared in *Agni, Michigan Quarterly Review, Ruminate,* and *The Baltimore Review.* His chapbook of translations from the German of Katharina Müller, *The Homeland,* is forthcoming from Cold Hub Press. You can read his occasional blog at matthewlandrum.com. He lives in Detroit.

**Thomas McClurg** has been pursuing the writing dream for the past 12 years. He loves to write fantasy and is in the process of shopping around a series of his novels. He had the chance to work briefly in television and draws much of his inspiration from movies and screenwriting.

He is a member of the Weaklings writers group and plays a part in putting on the Jot Writers' Conference each year. He has also spoken at other local writers' conferences in the Grand Rapids area. He currently lives in Grand Rapids with his wife, Amber. He can be found online at thomasmcclurg.com.

**Josh Mosey** is a husband, father, reader, writer, marketer, retailer, freelancer, Norse mythology enthusiast, Weaklings member, Jot Writers' Conference co-founder, Michigan native, conference speaker, book reviewer and publishing veteran. Like him on your favorite social media site or in real life or both. Josh occasionally updates his blog at joshmosey.com.

**Paul Kent Muckley** served as a non-fiction editor with Barbour Publishing, Inc., in Uhrichsville, Ohio, for 16 years before taking an editorial position with Discovery House in Grand Rapids, Michigan, in 2014. He also writes under the pseudonym Paul Kent, with a goal of making the Bible more interesting and accessible to readers of all ages and backgrounds. He has written eight books and contributed to approximately a dozen more.

**Amelia Rhodes** is the author of *Pray A to Z: A Practical Guide to Pray for Your Community* and *Isn't It Time for a Coffee Break: Doing Life Together in an All-About-Me Kind of World.* Amelia's writing has also been featured in four *Chicken Soup for the Soul* titles, in the international devotional *Upper Room,* and an upcoming devotional book from *Guideposts.* Amelia has a growing speaking ministry and speaks regularly on topics of spiritual growth, friendship and community, offering practical tools for living our faith in the everyday. She lives in Lowell, Michigan, with her husband and two children where she loves to hang out with friends over coffee. Connect with her online at ameliarhodes.com.

**A.L. Rogers** likes to write fiction, nonfiction and emails that are just a bit too long. His writing has appeared in *Splickety Magazine, Topology,* on DailyScienceFiction.com, and elsewhere. Andy has worked in the book industry since 2007 in retail, marketing and editing roles. He also helps organize the Jot Writers' Conference. Andy is married, a father, and lives in the Grand Rapids, Michigan area. Follow him on Twitter, @ALRstories.

**Tom Springer** lives in a farmhouse on four acres in Three Rivers, Michigan, which he shares with his wife, Nancy, and their two teenage daughters. His rural experiences with gardening, fishing, stargazing, beekeeping, "contemplative sloth" and renovation of a 19th home (which has a carbon footprint about the size of a small California town) often feature in his writing. A collection of Tom's essays, *Looking for Hickories* (University of Michigan Press, 2008), was named a Michigan Notable Book. Tom's essays have also appeared in publications such as *Notre Dame* magazine, *Michigan Out-of-Doors, Topology,* and *Dappled Things*, and aired as commentaries on National Public Radio programs. Tom worked for the W.K. Kellogg Foundation as a speechwriter, magazine editor and video producer, and is currently managing director of the Environmental Change Initiative at the University of Notre Dame.

**Ellen Stumbo** writes with gritty honesty and openness on issues of faith, disability, parenting and adoption. Ellen has written for the *Huffington Post, The Mighty, Charisma Magazine, Focus on the Family, Momsense,* LifeWay's ParentLife blog and magazine, and other publications. She is the Special Needs Ministry columnist for *Group* and the Special Needs Parenting columnist for *ParentLife*. Ellen is also a contributing writer to *Gifts 2: How People With Down Syndrome Enrich the World,* and the *SpiritLed Women's Bible*. She co-hosts a podcast called Unexceptional Moms: Hope and Encouragement for Special Needs Parents. Learn more about her writing and speaking at ellenstumbo.com.

**John Winkelman** is the chief operating officer of Caffeinated Press and the editor in chief of *The 3288 Review* literary journal. He has been involved in the West Michigan writing community since the late 1900s. He has been published in *Brewed Awakenings I* in 2015 and the 1999 issue of *Voices,* the annual journal of winners of the Dyer-Ives Poetry Competition. When not vetting and editing journal submissions he teaches tai chi and praying mantis kung fu in downtown Grand Rapids. He also has a day job.

# Acknowledgements
## A.L. Rogers

This book is a testament to what can happen when writers help other writers.

The well-worn maxim, *writing is a lonely business,* is true. But it doesn't have to be that way. In fact, I've learned that when writers choose to bring others into their world, they quickly find more success. They sharpen their craft because of the thoughtful critique others provide. They increase their number of publications because they have a group of people cheering them on to submit their work to publishers. And they find even greater joy in the writing process because they're surrounded by people who actually *get it.*

Writers may be stereotypically introverted, but that doesn't mean they don't need people.

Shortly after I decided to start writing, and before I even called myself a writer, I joined a writers' group. It remains one of the best decisions I have made. The five of us were all about the same age, living in the same geographic area, and we shared a passion for reading and dreams of writing. It was enough for us to pull together weekly meetings to talk about writing and see what might come of it.

While we had things in common, we weren't the same. Some wanted to write poetry, others epic fantasy. Some wanted to write for fun, while others dreamed of making their living as a professional writer. I knew, no matter what, I just wanted to become a better writer. And somehow I knew I needed a group of like-minded people to help me get there.

So without fanfare, but with plenty of junk food and bad puns, "The Weaklings" were born: a group of inexperienced writers just beginning their writing journey.

It was thrilling. We held our meetings in each other's apartments or sometimes the best faux English pub our Midwestern city had to offer. It was like being in a band. It was rock and roll.

Fast forward the story a few years and our writers' group decided that we wanted to do something bigger than us—bigger than just our normal meetings. We wanted to do something with other writers in the community. What that something was, we couldn't have told you, but that was when the first purple rays of this book started to glow on the horizon.

"Let's start a writers' conference!" someone said.

"That's so time-consuming," said another voice. "I barely have time to write, much less plan a conference."

"Besides," a third voice chimed in. "There's already a couple of writers' conferences in town. What could we offer that would be any different?"

Silence prevailed for a moment.

"And I don't have any time to write either. Not with work, the kids, and everything. And I certainly don't have any money to contribute to starting a conference."

(By the time of this conversation about half of our little band was married and starting to have young ones. Any of you who have lived with children know that they are a time and money vacuum.)

"That's it! That will be what makes us different! We'll put on a short conference—a *free, one-night* conference—that features really short workshops. We'll hold it somewhere with books and tables—like a bookstore—and *we'll build writing time into the conference schedule.* That will be our hook: Come to this conference. After all, it's free! Meet some people. Learn some stuff. And then spend some time *actually writing.*"

And thus, the Jot Writers' Conference was born.

Within a few months, our group hosted its first event for writers at a local bookstore. We invited other writers in the community to come give short talks about their craft, and then encouraged people to find cubby holes in the store to slip into with their journals or laptops for some writing time. If they didn't want to do that, they could always mingle with other writers by the coffee shop, or just walk around the bookstore. (And who doesn't love to walk around a bookstore?)

It was incredible. People actually came. Some folks wrote. Some folks gabbed over coffee. It was a smashing success.

This book is a product of those conferences. Nearly every contributor has been a speaker at a past Jot Writers' Conference. When our group had the idea of creating a book about writing it was a no-brainer to reach out to the vibrant community that has grown up around the Jot Writers'

Conference. And to my great joy, the community was excited about the idea too.

To each of those people, the contributors to this book as well as all of the other friends who have helped out with Jot, I want to say a sincere *thank you.* Writers need other writers to succeed. This book wouldn't have happened if my friends—this community of writers—hadn't caught the vision for sharing what they know in an effort to encourage other writers to succeed.

I cannot thank everyone by name, but a few people deserve special recognition. I hope that those I don't name individually will forgive me and believe me when I say I am deeply grateful for you too.

First, to Jason, John, AmyJo, and all the others at Caffeinated Press—thank you! What a joy it has been to work with you on this book. Thank you for giving so much of yourselves to writing and publishing.

To my brothers in the Weaklings, Bob, Josh, Matthew, and Thomas—look at this! Look at what we've done together! Thank you for your ideas, encouragement, and friendship. This book simply wouldn't exist without you all. Thank you, Matt and Bob, for getting this group started way back when.

To my wife, Kristen—what can I say? You did the dishes (again), took the trash out (again), did the laundry (again), put the kids to bed, skipped movies, stopped Netflix programs, took the kids to the store so I could have quiet, gave me full days off from work and parenting, and a thousand other little things *again and again and again,* all so I could work on the editing of this book. Thank you so much. I love you.

To all the past attendees of the Jot Writers' Conference and to any writer reading this—this book is for *you.*

You. Are. A. Writer.

It's really that simple. Jot that down and put it someplace where you'll see it every day. Now go write!

CPSIA information can be obtained
at www.ICGtesting.com
Printed in the USA
LVOW06s1327261017
553876LV00006B/82/P